D1458946

NEW DIRECTIONS
FOR CONTINUING
EDUCATION

Number 7 • 1980

NEW DIRECTIONS FOR CONTINUING EDUCATION

A Quarterly Sourcebook
Alan B. Knox, Editor-in-Chief

Number 7, 1980

Assessing Educational Needs of Adults

Floyd C. Pennington
Guest Editor

Jossey-Bass Inc., Publishers
San Francisco • Washington • London

ASSESSING EDUCATIONAL NEEDS OF ADULTS
New Directions for Continuing Education
Number 7, 1980
     Floyd C. Pennington, Guest Editor

New Directions for Continuing Education (publication number
0195-2242) quarterly by Jossey-Bass Inc., Publishers.
Subscriptions are available at the regular rate for institutions,
libraries, and agencies of $30 for one year. Individuals may
subscribe at the special professional rate of $18 for one year.

Correspondence:
Subscriptions, single-issue orders, change of address notices,
undelivered copies, and other correspondence should be sent to
New Directions Subscriptions, Jossey-Bass Inc., Publishers,
433 California Street, San Francisco, California 94104.

Editorial correspondence should be sent to the Editor-in-Chief,
Alan B. Knox, Office for the Study of Continuing Professional
Education, University of Illinois at Urbana–Champaign,
Urbana, Illinois 61801.

Library of Congress Catalogue Card Number LC 79-89390

Cover design by Willi Baum
Manufactured in the United States of America

Contents

Editor's Notes

The allocation of resources to specific programming activities is an important responsibility of continuing education practitioners. In any continuing education agency a substantial amount of attention is given to identifying and selecting ideas worth developing into programs and services. Increasing competition for a finite amount of resources points up the importance of identifying and assessing areas with the greatest potential for serving the needs of the client group as well as benefiting the continuing education agency. Needs assessment involves analyzing the gaps that exist between a present and a desired set of circumstances for adult learners.

The purposes of this sourcebook are to identify concepts and literature relevant to needs assessment, to show why assessment activities are important, to describe procedures for needs assessments in various settings, and to suggest useful and feasible approaches to needs assessment.

This volume is divided into three major sections. Chapter One, "Needs Assessment: Concepts, Models, and Characteristics," provides a basis for understanding how the term needs assessment has been used and critiques the major approaches taken in assessment activities.

Chapters Two through Eight describe needs assessment studies in various areas of continuing education fields. In "From Assessment to Implementation," Helen Veres describes a major effort by a state education department to conduct an assessment that would provide data to use in designing a statewide continuing education plan for adult learners. Robert Means, in the chapter "Comprehensive Statewide Needs Assessment of Community College Library Personnel," and Judith Fidler and David Loughran in "Systems Approach" describe studies for specific occupational groups that provided data to design subsequent training and development activities for association members and employees.

The chapters by Linda Bock and Linda Gunzburger describe the unique processes required to both assess the need for a specific program and at the same time acquire the requisite support from the organization and community for the programs.

In the chapters by Beverly Cassara and by Wayne Davis, Alan Hull, and Michele Boutagh studies of special client groups are described using two different developmental approaches to the assessment studies.

The last major section of the sourcebook discusses specific components of needs assessment studies as well as major issues to consider in embarking on assessment activities. In her chapter, Carolyn Barbulesco describes the characteristics of large-scale studies. Many of her specific suggestions can be used to design very modest assessment activities. Then, Phyllis Safman, in "Evaluating the Assessment: Did Anything Happen After We Left?", brings home the point that assessment without action is futile. She reminds the practitioner that just as plans for conducting the assessment are essential, plans for implementing and evaluating the results of the assessment cannot be neglected.

Finally, Don Moore reviews the studies described in this volume and summarizes, in a model, a reasoned approach to assessment activities. I conclude the volume by suggesting that a major lesson to be learned from these chapters is that assessments, simple or complex, are a valuable asset to the adult educator and require careful consideration as a source of decision-making information.

Floyd C. Pennington
Guest Editor

Floyd C. Pennington is director of the continuing medical education program at the University of Michigan in Ann Arbor. He spends a substantial amount of time on formal and informal needs assessment studies to provide a basis for sound program decision making.

*Sound approaches to needs assessment can assist practitioners in
using resources effectively to improve program decision making.
An overview of definitions, purposes, benefits, and models
provides a framework for the sourcebook and a foundation for
understanding needs assessment.*

Needs Assessment: Concepts, Models, and Characteristics

Floyd C. Pennington

Needs assessment as a basis for developing educational activities for adults has been called a difficult process surrounded by fuzzy thinking (Knox, 1969), the most persistent shibboleth in the rhetoric of adult education program planning (Griffith, 1978), the most ludicrous spectacle in evaluation (Scriven and Roth, 1978), the all-important first step in program development (Atwood and Ellis, 1971), and the bridge between recognizing a need and deciding what to do about it (Datta, 1978). Is this much disagreement inevitable? Can order be brought to this chaos? A major purpose of this sourcebook is to provide some form to the chaos by helping practitioners understand continuing education needs assessment and appreciate the potent contribution a systematic approach can offer for allocating the resources to plan, implement, and evaluate programming for adult learners. The sourcebook provides rationales and examples related to needs assessments to help practitioners understand, select, and use procedures of identifying, assessing, and making decisions about the educational needs of adult learners.

What constitutes need? Are educational needs different from other needs? How are needs related to interests, lacks, wants, social problems, goals, and deficiencies? Who is in the best position to identify the educational needs of individuals or groups? How can the continuing education practitioner effectively and efficiently identify, select, appraise, and act on adults' educational needs? Answers to these questions are addressed in this volume in the descriptions and discussion of systematic approaches to needs assessment.

The Definition of Need

One source of confusion regarding needs assessment is the lack of a generally accepted, useful, and substantive definition of need. Komisar (1961) suggests that the term survives because of its vagueness and multiplicity of meanings. Continuing education practitioners sometimes use the term merely to suggest that they are dealing with something essential for learners, rather than something self-serving. They use it in slogans and rhetoric to cultivate a supportive and committed environment and to give the appearance of insight and specificity while actually communicating little. The concept may be popular because it appears to emerge from empirical information that obviates the necessity for value judgments (Monette, 1977, 1979).

Atwood and Ellis (1971) suggest that a need is a deficiency that detracts from a person's well-being. Archambault (1957) uses the term to describe objectively demonstrable deficiencies of individuals in relation to their environments. Scriven and Roth (1978) express the idea that need is the gap between an actual and satisfactory situation and does not imply any state of deficiency or deprivation. Walton (1969) isolates four elements of a statement of needs: (1) a factual description of some empirically verifiable characteristic of an individual, (2) a comparison of this description with some desirable characteristic defined by an external criterion, (3) a conclusion that a change is desired, and (4) a strategy for satisfying the need through education.

It is useful to think of need as a gap between a current set of circumstances and some changed or desirable set of circumstances. The circumstances can be described in terms of proficiency (knowledge, skills, attitudes), performance, or situations. Needs can deal with desires, interests, or deficiencies. They can be specified for an individual or can be aggregated for groups, organizations, or the society. The changed set of circumstances can be described in terms of ways of altering the current situation.

Without comparison to a standard, it is difficult to examine a situation to determine demonstrable needs. Lacking comparative information, continuing education practitioners will impose their own values and perceptions on any set of data. There is a danger that continuing education practitioners, not always self-analytical, may assume that the needs they identify emerge directly from factual descriptions (Griffith, 1978). Monette (1979) has shown how practitioners' values and assumptions influence their thoughts about client needs.

Value judgments are unavoidable in educational needs assessments. Continuing education activities seek to help adults reflect on their thoughts and assumptions in relation to public thoughts and recognized knowledge. Program objectives typically include helping adults internalize new ideas to make them their own. Organized knowledge and espoused theory can serve such functions as exposing adult learners to broad social and ethical themes and validating their personal assumptions and experiences. This comparison of the personal with the situational can occur in needs assessments, as discrepancies between current and desired circumstances are analyzed.

For continuing professional education, Argyris and Schön (1976) have explained an approach to ongoing needs assessment that entails comparisons between espoused theory and theory-in-use. They have also developed a useful concept, termed "double loop" learning, in which a second "loop" involves reexamination of assumptions and values related to educational objectives. For example, in a competency-based educational program, this would mean discussing why the specific competences were chosen. Such consideration of assumptions and values is part of needs assessment as well as of learning activities.

Clarifying Assessment Purposes

Knowing why something is being done helps one to recognize when it is completed and what actions are required to reach completion. *Needs assessment* is a term that has been used to describe a process with at least three purposes, including analyzing clientele, identifying topics, and specifying areas of need. Analyzing characteristics and expectations of the clientele to provide data for program and policy decisions is common to each of these purposes.

Clientele analysis is the process of comparing the characteristics of the participants in continuing education programs with the characteristics of the general population of adults who could potentially be served. The characteristics compared typically include age, sex, education, marital status, occupation, recency of participation in a formal educational activity, and other variables correlated with participation in continuing education activities.

The second major set of activities in needs assessment involves identifying areas of demand for educational programming. For some continuing education agencies this is part of market research. To maintain viability, continuing education agencies must attract resources, convert these resources into programs and services, and distribute these benefits to consuming publics. Estimates of demand for programs in relation to programs of other providers are used in setting program priorities. The continuing education agency relies on offering programs and services of sufficient interest to elicit active participation (Kotler, 1975).

The third major activity under the needs assessment umbrella consists of attempts to identify discrepancies between a current and a desired set of circumstances. These activities include techniques of identifying and understanding problem areas. Data are collected and comparisons made. The result of these activities is careful definition of a gap or problem, including its magnitude, components, and intensity.

Data obtained from these three activities require analysis and action to be useful for program development decisions. Without the analysis, needs assessment is not complete. All three types of information are important. Which to emphasize depends on the reasons for collecting the information.

Nowlen (1980) has provided a useful rationale for determining needs assessment purposes by reviewing the types of information that continuing education practitioners can use to originate new programs. Illustrative sources include research findings about adult development (Knox, 1979b), questionnaire responses from clientele surveys, and evidence about emerging societal trends. He concluded that in the priority-setting process information about educational needs is usually screened in relation to agency purposes and resources, along with the offerings of other providers. In this context, a main reason for needs assessment is to identify promising ideas for new or modified programs so that they are responsive to current or new categories of clients. This approach can be especially helpful for continuing education providers such as school systems or community colleges that are oriented toward service to a broad cross-section of adults in a geographic area.

By contrast, in continuing professional education a clientele such as members of a professional association may be a "given," and the purpose of a needs assessment may be to identify salient and emerging needs on which to focus more attention (Le Breton, 1979). Especially in technical fields, concepts of obsolescence and proficiency, along with personal and situational influences on performance, can help focus a needs assesssment study (Knox, 1979a). Sometimes attention to a professional field and to a geographic area are combined, as in the study of educational needs of physicians in Utah (Storey, Williamson, and Castle, 1978).

Information about needs assessment also indicates the survival of externally funded continuing education projects. (Farmer and Knox, 1977). A national study of projects designed to improve community problem solving revealed that more projects that used formal needs assessment procedures than that used informal estimates helped to strengthen institutional capability to provide continuing education and community service and continued beyond the period of external funding from Title I of the Higher Education Act of 1965. Informal methods included brief checklists completed by a sample of clients and samples of faculty members' opinions about what clients needed.

Campbell (1980) suggests that formal needs assessments are more warranted when the beneficiaries of continuing education extend beyond the individual to include people associated with a group, organization, or community than when the main purpose of the program is self-enrichment. For example, when a company conducts an in-service education program to improve job performances, organizational expectations are important and supervisors may be a crucial source of needs assessment information.

It is important, however, to remember that only individuals have educational needs, learn, and apply what they learn. In this sense, groups, organizations, and communities do not have educational needs. They have problems and opportunities for which education may be needed. Certain individual educational needs may be widespread within such groups. Because individuals interact in such settings, they have educational needs related to interpersonal relations and collective issues, but it is not the group, organization, or community that has an educational need. If the main purpose of needs assessment is to make continuing education programs responsive to adult learners, this is an important distinction to keep in mind. It is especially important when the program's purpose is to benefit problem solving related to the quality of collective life. However, this distinction in no way reduces the importance of collecting needs assessment data from people from various role perspectives in a group, organization, or community.

Models of Needs Assessment

Needs assessment models vary in purpose, scope, and magnitude. Six general clusters of models can be identified in the literature. McKinley (1973) identified three clusters of needs assessment models: individual self-fulfillment models, individual appraisal models, and system discrepancy models. Three additional clusters have been described by others: diagnostic models, analytic models, and democratic models.

1. The *self-fulfillment* cluster includes random and selective appeal models. Random appeals aim at discovering those needs (usually defined as interests or wants) of a large segment of the population that are potent enough to attract them to educational activities and make a program financially self-supporting. They appeal to individual and not community needs. Selective appeals focus on the presumed needs of a known segment of the population (professionals, the underemployed, the aged). Programs based on this model generally use formats that have already been tested with the specialized population. The problems with these approaches are lack of measurement precision, planner and institutional bias in analyzing results, and the tendency toward creating and maintaining a market rather than focusing on learning needs.

2. *Individual appraisals* engage the participation of individual learners in determining their own learning needs, either collaboratively or noncollaboratively. In the collaborative model the learner uses the assistance of others in clarifying needs. In the noncollaborative or self-appraisal model learners choose

assessment techniques to measure their own learning needs. The problems with these models are the potential lack of vision on the part of the learner in recognizing and understanding essential learning needs; the biases built into measurement instruments, which may not be related to individuals' actual circumstances; and dependence on individual initiative for specification and follow-up.

3. The *system discrepancy* cluster includes models that seek to identify the gaps between what is and what ought to be in a given situation. The problem-need approaches attempt to define deficiencies and then develop remedial programs. Educational needs and educational objectives are directly related to diagnosed difficulties in the client system. Goal-identification approaches result in educational programs with a general improvement thrust rather than a specific remedial focus. They assume that educational objectives that are carefully derived from the goals of the client system (for example, the medical profession) will reflect desired learning outcomes (such as improved patient care) that some educators would term needs.

4. The *diagnostic or medical model* views need as something whose absence or deficiency proves harmful. In the simplest case, the practitioner identifies a need by observing what happens when adults are deprived of a resource and then projects what would happen if they had that resource. This approach searches for both met and unmet needs and uses available knowledge and logic to decide which deficiencies would be harmful. Needs specified using the diagnostic model can be more precisely described in terms of a performance deficit and in terms of a treatment deficit. The former is illustrated by the assertion, "Physicians need to achieve mastery of cardiopulmonary resuscitation before they receive their license to participate in continuing medical education programs." Treatment needs that are broadly described are poorly related to feasible actions, while performance-deficit needs statements give no intrinsic guidance to what treatment is needed.

5. The *analytic model* defines a direction in which improvement would occur, given information about the status of a person or a program. It places a premium on informed judgment and systematic problem solving. It seeks full description of the thing or person whose needs are being assessed. It focuses on improvement rather than remediation and does not require advance statements of standards or success criteria. Two problems with this approach are that it is an abstraction that may be difficult to apply and requires skilled problem solvers.

6. The *democratic model* involves interactive and collaborative efforts at specifying needs using nomination and voting techniques. Nominal group processes and *delphi* techniques (Delbecq and others, 1975) exemplify this approach. The problems with this model are the possibility that the required consensus may discourage dealing with critical issues and that progress in reducing dissonance in the population may be impeded by waiting for majority approval.

These six models of needs assessment indicate the general approaches that have been used. Practitioners who want to conduct a needs assessment can use this typology to help locate studies on desired approaches.

Practicality May Help

Why assess needs? Because data is needed to make decisions that have an impact on the continuing education agency. The common thread tying together the theory and practice of needs assessment may be that these studies, however modest, are conducted to provide data for making informed and responsive programming decisions. Effective needs assessment studies are rational responses to identified problems, designed to suggest alternative solutions to those problems and to provide the requisite information, so that action decisions can be made. Continuing education practitioners do not have the resources or patience to engage in needs assessment studies that do not provide adequate information for the essential decision making related to their programming efforts. As practical activities, needs assessments should help practitioners understand the problems being assessed, be clear about their task, plan for the execution of the study, and know how the results will be useful before a study is initiated. Needs assessment studies start from an informed base and proceed in logical and sequential steps to plan, implement, report, and use the data from the investigation. Two excellent resources that provide detailed practical guidance to persons conducting needs assessments are Barbulesco (1976) and Witken (1975). Many of the ideas in the sections that follow are taken from these two resources.

Continuing education practitioners might well spend a quarter of the total time required to conduct a needs assessment in planning for the execution of the study. During the planning phase answers might be sought to the following questions:

- Who is the audience that will be using the needs assessment data as an input into their decision making? (Administrators, teachers, learners, policy makers)
- What questions do these persons need answered so that informed judgments and clear action plans can be made? (This conclusion should help set the scope of the study)
- What data will the decision maker trust?
- Do the data exist? How accessible are the data?
- What techniques should be employed to acquire the essential data?
- How do the decision makers want the data presented?

What should the continuing education practitioner expect in return for the investment made in a carefully conceived systematic needs assessment? Some potential benefits include:

- Data to use in implementing positive changes in educational programs

- A clearer understanding of changing patterns of educational needs
- Data for making decisions about programming priorities to use in selecting new programs
- An information base for deciding about resource allocation
- An expanding empirical data base for future decisions regarding educational programs or policy
- Data regarding learner preferences for content areas and instructional styles
- Data to focus programs so that purposes and intended consequences are an integral part of the programs' design deliberations
- Increases in public involvement and commitment to educational planning and participation
- Responses to federal and state mandates requiring appropriate use of public monies

Needs assessment studies have several major characteristics. Most needs assessments employ a systematic method of collecting data from persons who can affect or are affected by the problem being examined (Witken, 1975). A second characteristic is that needs assessments are continuous (Atwood and Ellis, 1971; Kaufman, 1972; Watson, 1973). Needs of constituent groups are not fixed over time, but change as preferences and environments change. Continuous assessments can help monitor these changes to assure that data being used to make programming decisions are relevant to the problem and the client.

Needs assessments vary in scope and cost (Knox, 1978). Data can be collected systematically by making a few phone calls to key persons in a constituent group. Studies can involve a variety of data collection techniques and include many persons in the study. Studies can be included in a person's job responsibilities or can be major projects funded by an external agency, staffed by a core of researchers skilled in needs assessment studies. Assessment studies can be done within organizations, communities, states, or on a national scale.

The needs assessment studies reviewed by Cross (1979), for example, were mainly statewide studies that produced findings so consistent that Cross questioned the need for further replication. This type of large, formal study was also conducted by Hamilton (1976). By contrast, most continuing education needs assessments are conducted by a program administrator with very little time or money. This occurs when a conference coordinator assembles a planning committee composed of both potential participants and experts and explores ideas about relating programs to client needs with them. Modest needs assessment also occurs when an association executive selects a small but representative sample of members at a national conference and asks each person about the unmet educational needs that could be responded to in the next program.

Campbell (1980) prepared a pamphlet that can help practitioners conduct needs assessments. One section lists major contributions of various sources of information about educational needs. For example, information from potential participants helps to ensure program relevance and stimulates their interest in the program, while a review of professional literature can identify professional trends and controversies. The pamphlet also analyzes sources of information about needs in relation to program type, scope, history, intended audience, and available resources for conducting studies. Campbell reviews strengths and weaknesses of various data collection methods and suggests methods that are best in relation to program type, scope of needs assessment, and clientele characteristics. For example, questionnaires are relatively inexpensive to administer but are impersonal and yield limited information. By contrast, group interviews require less time and money than personal interviews, but data analysis can be difficult and time-consuming. The following comparisons illustrate criteria for selecting data collection methods: For an informal needs assessment for a self-enrichment program for adults with low educational levels who are scattered over a large geographic area, brief telephone interviews with a small but representative sample of potential participants is the preferred data-collection method. By contrast, for an extensive needs assessment for a career development program for professional personnel in one company, where success is especially important, the preferred data-collection method would be a combination of individual interviews with potential participants, group interviews with their supervisors, and questionnaires for experts.

Data collected in needs assessments can be both subjective and objective. Continuing education practitioners will be interested in opinions as well as quantitative indices describing the extent and dimensions of the problem being examined. Each practitioner will value different data and weigh these data accordingly in their decisions. For some, the objective data will weigh more heavily than the subjective data. For others, the opinions and conjectures of the client group will be more relevant for decision making. In most cases, a combination of data sources will provide a more reasonable basis for making programming decisions than will a single source.

Because of the widespread use of modest surveys to collect needs assessment data, efforts to increase the importance and clarity of the items used in a questionnaire or interview guide could greatly improve current practice. The following examples illustrate some of the better items currently in use: The typical core of an educational needs assessment survey is a list of proficiencies that respondents rate according to how much time they would spend learning more about each. The types of proficiencies listed are specific to the clientele to be surveyed. For example, a survey of illiterate and unemployed young adults might emphasize topics related to reading, math, health, consumer decisions, and finding work. A survey of electrical engineers might emphasize highly specialized tasks and new developments in the field. A survey of residents of a community college district might emphasize a wide range of more general topics. The list of topics is representative rather than comprehensive, and consists of phrases such as: "supervise employees with attention to their satisfaction as well as meeting organizational goals," "speak another language well enough to travel and shop," "handle family finances so income buys more of what members want," "write satisfactory reports," "understand ways to improve relations between parents and their teenagers." The heading for the list might ask the respondents to check how much time he or she would be interested in spending to learn more about each topic. The response categories might be "none," "less than ten hours," "ten-forty hours," and "more than forty hours."

Another aspect of needs assessment concerns the benefits that adults hope to obtain from continuing education. The heading of a list of reasons for participation might say, "Please check how important each of the following reasons for participation in educational activities is to you." The response categories might be "none," "some," "much." Examples of benefits include: "to help me achieve a goal for others," "to compare viewpoints with other adults interested in a topic," "to find out about new knowledge and developments," "to review what I first learned years ago," and "to enjoy mental stimulation."

For participants in current programs, a question could be asked, "What additional topics would you like to study in the future?" The current program topic provides a common starting point for thinking about follow-up topics, whereas for a survey of the general public it is better to provide a list of possible topics. Most surveys also ask a few questions about characteristics of respondents, such as age, educational level, and occupational specialization or work arrangement, to help interpret responses about needs. Many surveys also ask respondents about preferences for season of the year, days of the week, times of the day, and schedule of sessions during which a program would be held.

A pervasive characteristic of most needs assessments resulting in effective action is the involvement of potential participants, community groups, and educators as partners in decision making. Needs assessment studies involving persons carefully selected for their role perspectives on the problem being assessed can build support for the study, for the decisions made during the study, and for subsequent programs or services that follow the assessment. Multiple role perspectives enrich the deliberations about the problem and the development of alternative solutions. Decision makers feel more comfortable in selecting courses of action if representatives of persons who are required to carry out the action are brought into the assessment activity from its inception.

Finally, a needs assessment is a transitional process from the present to the future. Needs assessment studies are systematic attempts to observe a current set of circumstances and to project a more desired set of circumstances. Results from needs assessment studies provide both (1) baseline data for making summative evaluation judgments regarding program impact, and (2) planning data for projecting alternative mechanisms to reduce the gap between current and desired circumstances. This developmental quality of needs assessment makes it important for practitioners to understand major concepts about adult development (Knox, 1977). Such understanding can help practitioners to anticipate the educational needs of adults undergoing major role changes, for example, and to reflect this understanding in efforts to attract people with a heightened readiness to learn, in relevant instructional activities, and in evaluation activities for assessing program impact on performance.

Subsequent chapters provide guidelines for conducting major needs assessment studies. Needs assessment procedures should be influenced by the type of questions that need to be asked about the problem, the data collection technique selected, and the requirements of the persons to whom the data will be reported. Following are some general suggestions that might be useful in planning for and implementing a major needs assessment study:

1. Make sure someone is responsible for the study and that there is support from the organization's administrative structure. Someone must see to it that the study's details are taken care of and the organization must be committed to conducting the study and using the results.

2. Make sure the key people in the agency know about the study and how outcomes might benefit their efforts.

3. Ask questions about the problem in a variety of ways. Use different methods and techniques to gather information. Obtain data from a variety of people with independent perspectives on the problem.

4. Be clear about the information that you are requesting from people. Avoid ambiguous directions and make sure the respondents understand the questions.

5. Be sensitive to the pressures and constraints on people responding to the assessment. Be prepared to revisit persons who cannot take adequate time to participate.

6. Do not raise people's expectations by requesting information that you cannot use or encourage others to use.

7. Be aware that people are expecting something to occur after an assessment and that they will be looking for things they thought were important.

8. Use existing data sources where possible. If someone has gathered all or part of the information you need, use what you can from those efforts. Such sources as previous unpublished studies, public documents, and published literature should be examined first. This will help keep your study manageable.

9. Establish ground rules early. Who will have access to the data? When can they have access? What can they use the data for prior to the completion of the study?

10. Have a rationale for all the data you collect. Needs assessment studies are intended to support specific decisions. Do not take the attitude, "While I'm doing this I might as well get all I can from these people."
11. Be ready to respond to unintended outcomes. The study design should not serve as blinders. Excellent input may be acquired from unexpected quarters. Be flexible enough to pursue leads where appropriate.
12. Delineate options and provide supportive data for decision makers, but let them do the deciding.
13. Provide feedback to appropriate persons throughout the study. In some instances, preliminary data may be required before you intended to make it available. Be sure that the data released is as carefully considered as possible and that contingencies are clearly specified if early reporting is required.
14. Be professional in the conduct of your study. Show that you know what you are doing and that actions will follow the study.
15. Be tolerant of ambiguity when the responses you get are not really answers to the questions you asked. You may not get answers to all of your questions or have an opportunity to ask all of the questions.
16. Share your plan for the study with others to see if it makes sense. Test your questions with small numbers of respondents before undertaking a large-scale study. Be prepared with queries and ways of analyzing results before the study is under way.
17. Express appreciation to those participating in the study. In many instances these are potential clients.
18. Don't expect the program that is designed following a needs assessment study to be one that you think you could have proposed beforehand.
19. Get all the mileage you can from the data. Analyze and reanalyze. The more ways you examine the data, the more valuable insights can be found.

Following these suggestions will not guarantee successful needs assessment studies. They do, however, reflect the common sense and courtesy that is an ally to a needs assessment study and to the decisions based on study outcomes. Most continuing education practitioners cannot conduct a comprehensive needs assessment for every new educational activity and service planned by their organization. The realities of staff, time, and money are restrictive. Some assessment, however, can be done for every program and service an agency is considering. This is especially true for proposed programs for which the cost of an unsuccessful effort would be high. From small, informed queries to expansive studies, reasonable data for decisions can be acquired and should play an important role in educational planning for continuing education programs and services.

References

Archambault, R. D. "The Concept of Need and Its Relation to Certain Aspects of Education Theory." *Harvard Education Review,* 1957, *27,* 38–62.

Argyris, C., and Schön, D. A. *Theory in Practice: Increasing Professional Effectiveness.* San Francisco: Jossey-Bass, 1974.

Atwood, H. M., and Ellis, J. "The Concept of Need: An Analysis for Adult Education." *Adult Leadership,* 1971, *19,* 210–212, 244.

Barbulesco, C. "Educational Needs Assessment Related to Community Problem Solving Programs in Higher Education: Theory and Practice." Unpublished master's thesis, University of Illinois at Urbana–Champaign, 1976.

Campbell, M. D. *Before You Plan Educational Programs: Find Out What's Needed.* Office of Continuing Education and Public Service, University of Illinois at Urbana–Champaign, 1980.

Cross, K. P., and Zusman, A. "The Needs of Non-Traditional Learners and the Responses of Non-Traditional Programs." In C. B. Stalford (Ed.), *An Evaluative Look at Non-Traditional Education.* Washington, D.C.: National Institute of Education, 1979.

Datta, L. "Front-End Analysis: Pegasus or Shank's Mare?" In S. B. Anderson and C. D. Coles (Eds.), *New Directions for Program Evaluation: Exploring Purposes and Dimensions,* no. 1. San Francisco: Jossey-Bass, 1978.

Delbecq, A. L., and others. *Group Techniques for Program Planning: A Guide to Nominal Group and Delphi Processes.* Glenview, Ill.: Scott, Foresman, 1975.

Farmer, J. A., Jr., and Knox, A. B. *Alternative Patterns for Strengthening Community Service Programs in Institutions of Higher Education.* Urbana: University of Illinois, 1977.

Griffith, W. S. "Educational Needs: Definition, Assessment, and Utilization." *School Review,* 1978, pp. 382–384.

Hamilton, I. B. *The Third Century: Postsecondary Planning for the Non-Traditional Learner.* Princeton, N.J.: Educational Testing Service, 1976.

Kaufman, R. A. *Educational System Planning.* Englewood Cliffs, N.J.: Prentice Hall, 1972.

Knox, A. B. "Critical Appraisal of the Needs of Adults for Education Experiences as a Basis for Program Development." New York: Adult Education Department, Teachers College, Columbia University, 1969. (ERIC document ED 022 090)

Knox, A. B. *Adult Development and Learning.* San Francisco: Jossey-Bass, 1977.

Knox, A. B. *Helping Adults to Learn.* Concept Paper No. 4. Washington, D.C.: The Continuing Library Education Network and Exchange, 1978.

Knox, A. B. "The Nature and Causes of Professional Obsolescence." In P. P. Le Breton and Associates (Eds.), *The Evaluation of Continuing Education for Professionals: A Systems View.* Seattle: Continuing Education, University of Washington, 1979a.

Knox, A. B. (Ed.) *New Directions for Continuing Education: Programming for Adults Facing Mid-Life Change,* no. 2. San Francisco: Jossey-Bass, 1979b.

Komisar, B. P. " 'Need' and the Needs Curriculum." In B. O. Smith and R. H. Ennis (Eds.), *Language and Concepts in Education.* Chicago: Rand McNally, 1961.

Kotler, P. *Marketing for Nonprofit Organizations.* Englewood Cliffs, N.J.: Prentice-Hall, 1975.

Le Breton, P. P., and Associates (Eds.). *The Evaluation of Continuing Education for Professionals: A Systems View.* Seattle: Continuing Education, University of Washington, 1979.

McKinley, J. "Perspectives on Diagnostics in Adult Education." *Viewpoints, Bulletin of the School of Education, Indiana University,* 1973, *49* (5), 69–83.

Monette, M. L. "The Concept of Education Need: An Analysis of Selected Literature." *Adult Education,* 1977, *27* (2), 116–127.

Monette, M. L. "Need Assessment: A Critique of Philosophical Assumptions." *Adult Education,* 1979, *29* (2), 83–95.

Nowlen, P. M. "Origins." In A. B. Knox (Ed.), *Developing, Administering, and Evaluating Adult Education.* San Francisco: Jossey-Bass, 1980.

Scriven, M., and Roth, J. "Needs Assessment: Concept and Practice." In S. B. Anderson and C. D. Coles (Eds.), *New Directions for Program Evaluation: Exploring Purposes and Dimensions,* no. 1. San Francisco: Jossey-Bass, 1978.

Storey, P. B., Williamson, J. W., and Castle, C. H. *Continuing Medical Education.* Chicago: American Medical Association, 1968.

Walton, R. "Need: A Central Concept." *Social Service Quarterly,* 1969, *43,* 13–17.

Watson, C. D. *Educational Needs Assessment.* Little Rock: Arkansas Department of Education, 1973. (ERIC document ED 084 293)

Witkin, B. R. *An Analysis of Needs Assessment Techniques for Educational Planning at State, Intermediate and District Levels.* Washington, D.C.: National Institute of Education, Department of Health, Education and Welfare, 1975.

Floyd C. Pennington is director of the continuing medical education program at the University of Michigan at Ann Arbor. He spends a substantial amount of time on formal and informal needs assessment studies to provide a basis for sound program decision making.

Gathering information is futile without implementation
of programs based on the findings.

From Assessment
to Implementation

Helen C. Veres

Needs assessments have widespread appeal for educators today. Most administrators and planners who grapple with problems of designing effective and responsive programs, allocating scarce resources, and setting educational policies now seem to rely on needs assessments in making difficult decisions.

Problems facing continuing educators often contrast sharply with those confronting administrators in schools and colleges serving youth. Participation of adults in educational activities has grown rapidly, while enrollments at other educational levels have plummeted. Between 1969 and 1975, national continuing education enrollments increased by 31 percent—two and one-half times faster than the increase in the adult population (Boaz, 1978). In New York State alone, enrollment figures for public continuing education in the first seven years of the decade increased by over two hundred thousand persons to a total of nearly one million.

While such impressive growth rates would hardly seem cause for complaint by educators, satisfaction is often tempered by the knowledge that large numbers of people still do not participate in any type of organized learning. In fact, despite the dramatic growth, the National Center for Education Statistics data (Boaz, 1978) indicate that only about one in ten adults (11.6 percent) participates in organized instruction. (The data-collection procedures probably underestimate actual participation rates.) Although many other adults learn through self-directed or other informal efforts (Tough, 1978), studies of participation in continuing education continue to show that certain groups enroll disproportionately in organized educational activities (Carp, Peterson, and Roelfs, 1974; Johnstone and Rivera, 1965). Because participants are more likely than nonparticipants to be well-off economically and educationally, there is concern that the educational needs of a large proportion of adults are not being adequately served.

Evidence exists that nearly all adults may be considered potential participants (Tough, 1978), but clearly many do not or cannot take advantage of existing opportunities. The improvement of continuing education services depends, in part, upon an exchange of information between learners and providers of adult learning activities. This flow of information is complex; it involves such factors as the participants' potential awareness of their educational needs and interests and the existence of appropriate activities to satisfy those needs. Similarly, those who provide continuing education require current and detailed information about potential participants in order to make program and policy decisions. They also must bring present and proposed program offerings to the attention of potential clients. In this process, adequate information is an essential link between the decisions of learners and of providers of services.

The Need for Information

In New York State, the Division of Continuing Education of the State Education Department recognizes that detailed information is a necessary first step for improving the delivery of continuing education services. The State Education Department provides direct assistance and coordination to a portion of the state's providers—the nearly five hundred public educational institutions comprised of public schools, boards of cooperative educational services and public two-year colleges. However, there exists within the state a vast array of learning resources, including educational institutions, community organizations, businesses, home-instruction services, and others. Even the most conscientious continuing education administrators find it difficult to stay up-to-date on the variety of learning opportunities available in their communities, much less to coordinate their services with others. To complicate matters, nearly two-thirds of program administrators perform their professional responsibilities part-time. They have little time for mandated activities, however desirable.

These conditions, combined with practitioner interest in better information about the needs of adult learners and the available services, resulted in a comprehensive study, funded under the Adult Education Act, Title VI, to supply improved information for continuing education planning. The study involved extensive data collection to assess the continuing education needs of

New York State adults, to examine the state's present delivery system for continuing education, and to assess the in-service education needs of continuing education faculty and administrators. These three sources of information would be used to assist in making state and local decisions.

Planning the Assessment

Planning, to be done well, takes time and effort. What information is actually needed? Why? What form would facilitate later use of the information? How will results be implemented?

In the case of the New York state assessment, the persons responsible for implementing results were involved in answering these basic questions. Initially, state-level administrators outlined their interests in obtaining baseline information about adult learning interests and barriers that was comparable across the state. Then local program administrators were invited to request more detailed information about the learning preferences of adults in their communities. While differences in perception sometimes necessitated compromise on the type and extent of information to be gathered, consensus was obtained on a variety of basic issues.

First, it was agreed that the general population of adults should be surveyed. Personal interviews would supply the most useful data for planners. In addition, because results were intended for decision makers at the regional and subregional levels, data would be analyzed to address local planning needs. These decisions resulted in a large survey population, requiring considerable time and effort to obtain the necessary information. The assessment thus depended on cooperation among a variety of individuals, who assisted in all phases of the project. They ranged from professional educators to lay citizens and included representatives of state and local educational institutions, the state education department, and community agencies.

The involvement of many individuals in various roles across a wide geographic area multiplied difficulties in coordination and communication. Nevertheless, direct contact through the data-collection process with a wide spectrum of individuals, from members of the target audience to program administrators, helped create an informed group with greater commitment to using the study results. Representation by a cross-section of institutions and agencies offering continuing education services provided opportunities for greater contact and increased coordination of services.

A State Education Department staff member was selected as project manager. In addition, three other institutions were involved in implementing various tasks of the study. Because of previous experience in conducting studies of adult needs, the Institute for Occupational Education at Cornell University planned and administered the survey of adults. The Office of Research and Evaluation Services of the City College of New York collected and analyzed data for New York City. Related activities, including a staff development survey and project information workshops, were carried out by the Two-Year College Development Center at the State University of New York at Albany. Each university unit had a separate project director and staff members. Scheduled meetings coordinated the various parts of the project.

The Management Plan

The vast amount of local data to be gathered, while keeping the project cost-effective, necessitated a management strategy that involved an alliance of local school districts, Boards of Cooperative Educational Services (BOCES) and two-year colleges. Because the State Education Department was the project sponsor and in its official capacity maintained contact with administrators in local school districts, this existing structure was employed. This facilitated the participation of many professional educators, while avoiding creation of a costly new structure to administer the needs assessment survey.

Since New York City has its own administrative structure for education and contains almost half of the state's population in a limited geographic area, special attention was focused on the problems of obtaining data from this large, high-density population. As a result, the study was carried out in two stages: (1) a survey of Regions One through Nine, followed by (2) a survey only of Region Ten, New York City.

In the study, the forty-five supervisory districts in Regions One through Nine and the thirty-two community school districts in New York City formed the smallest reporting units. This structure officially applies to the administration of public schools within the state; however, for study purposes, two-year colleges located within each district were included. In each region, a manager was appointed to supervise the survey. These managers were usually directors of local programs who had shown deep interest in the development of continuing education and who possessed leadership and managerial capabilities. Each regional manager developed a "cabinet," a committee representing school districts within the region. Committee members were chosen from local directors of continuing education in public schools and BOCES facilities, as well as from deans of continuing education in public two-year colleges. The members of these communities in turn worked with other program directors at the local community level. In school districts not offering continuing education, the director of continuing education of the BOCES of another member of the committee acquainted the chief school officer with the project and sought cooperation.

Management responsibilities included identifying volunteer interviewers to conduct the survey; training those volunteers; and distributing, collecting, and returning survey materials. Each regional manager administered a small budget ($1,500) to cover such necessary expenses as transportation to cabinet meetings, office supplies, and other special costs.

In New York City there are no supervisory districts. The project director and staff there assumed many of the duties of the regional manager, including interviewer training and the organization of meetings.

The Survey

Instrumentation. In the fall of 1975, an instrument to survey adults' perceived learning needs was developed and field-tested by staff of the Institute for Occupational Education at Cornell University. This instrument was constructed to elicit data closely comparable with other regional and national studies of continuing education, such as the national data gathered in 1972 by the Commission on Non-Traditional Study (Carp, Peterson, and Roelfs, 1974) and the regional studies conducted in New York State with funds from Title I of the Higher Education Act of 1976. The instrument was designed to obtain information from personal interviews covering several major topics:

- Background information on the adults surveyed
- Past participation in continuing education
- Expressed learning interests
- Obstacles to participation in continuing education
- Preferred conditions for participation in continuing education
- Potential for use of counseling and advising services for adults

Questions were constructed in a multiple choice format, with answers to be recorded on a machine-scorable form. The majority of these questions had precoded response categories. Options such as "other" or "don't know" were included to allow for answers not specified among the choices. A summary sheet allowed the interviewer to record other comments or special information from the survey participant, for example, reasons for incomplete interviews, or number of persons who declined to be interviewed. This was considered the most effective way of handling the vast amount of survey data while recording special circumstances.

The questionnaire was reviewed by continuing education professionals and program administrators across the state. Special attention was devoted to identifying problems in the wording of questions and response categories, clarity and sequencing of questions, and adaptability to the various geographic areas of the state. Minor revisions were made in the questionnaire as a result.

Next, a pilot test of the instrument was conducted in the central portion of the state with some fifty adults of various ages and educational backgrounds, to identify additional problems with questionnaire content or method. Several further revisions were made in the wording of questions and responses. An estimate of the time required for interviews was also obtained, the average being about one-half hour.

This process was repeated in the second stage to adapt the survey instrument for use in New York City. Several questions were modified to reflect urban conditions, especially in transportation. Translations of the instrument into Spanish and ten other foreign languages allowed interviews to be conducted with large ethnic populations.

Interviewer Selection and Training. Collecting data throughout New York State made it necessary to train large numbers of interviewers. The regional manager, advisory cabinet members, and local directors of continuing education identified potential interviewers. They considered whether the interviewer was representative of the population to be interviewed, familiar with the area, mature and responsible, fluent in a foreign language where appropriate, and willing to be trained.

Throughout the state approximately 2,200 persons were identified and trained as interviewers. In the initial phase all interviewers volunteered eight to ten unpaid hours of time on behalf of the local continuing education program. The second phase, in New York City, required a greater time commitment from interviewers and a small honorarium compensated them for the additional effort.

Each interviewer was required to attend a detailed local training session on interviewing techniques. At each session, the purpose and general procedures for the survey were explained. Trainees were provided with sets of questionnaires, written instructions on administration of the interviews, additional instruction about their assignments, and practice materials. In order to ensure maximum cooperation from community residents, interviewers were also given an identification card, endorsed by the local chief school officer, stating the interviewer's name and the purpose of the survey. Regional team members were also asked to publish information about the needs assessment in local newspapers or school newsletters before actual interviews.

The Sample of Adults

The population to be interviewed included all persons age sixteen or older not currently full-time students. Individuals were to be interviewed from each school district with varying numbers of interviews assigned, depending upon population. A minimum of 350 interviews was sought from each supervisory or community school district so that local findings could be adequately reported.

Regional managers and teams were furnished with detailed census information about residents of the area's school districts. To avoid extensive, time-consuming travel, interviews were apportioned in clusters of five. Using the official census or school district map, these clusters were randomly distributed within the school district.

Interviewers were given other special instructions. They were instructed to alternate interviews between males and females and to conduct interviews at different times of day. In several districts with large non-English-speaking populations, bilingual interviews were used.

This approach resulted in a total of 28,615 usable interviews out of a state population of 10.4 million persons aged twenty-five and over (57 percent of the 1970 census population) who constituted a potential audience for continuing education services.

Data Analysis. Meeting the specific learning needs of a particular adult is a difficult task. Since adulthood encompasses about two-thirds of the average life span, the adult population consists of individuals with diverse characteristics and with differing perceptions of why and what they want to learn, as well as with different learning styles and basic abilities. Individuals may, however, share similar learning needs with others of like sex, age, educational background, or other common characteristics, so the interview data were analyzed for various sub-groups. Analyses were based upon the earlier planning questions posed by state and local administrators. What do adults want to learn? Where do they want to study? Are present services meeting current adult needs?

Reporting the Results. Educators must be aware of information about the needs of adult learners in order to respond adequately. Disseminating information is thus a necessary part of needs assessments. Since lengthy printed reports are often overlooked or do not reach decision-makers, extensive dissemmination was essential for results of the needs assessment to be applied in the field. This included consultation services as well as workshops and meetings where time was allotted for discussing state and regional data.

The intention was to reach as many people as possible across the state, particularly those responsible for adult and continuing education programs. Throughout the process, regional organizations developed during data collection completed regional reports of needs assessment data to serve as regional planning bases. Continuing educators from public schools, boards of cooperative educational services, and community colleges were encouraged to maintain these coordinating organizations.

Several workshops acquainted management teams with findings and initiated work on a summary report of needs assessment findings and their regional implications. These were followed a few months later by a workshop in each region. Each regional workshop opened with a dinner to which state and local decision makers were invited — including members of the state board of regents, state legislature, local elected officials, local school district board members, school superintendents, and college and university administrators, as well as representatives of local news media, cooperative extension services, library services, and community and service organizations interested in educational services for adults.

Results of the Needs Assessment

Information generated from over twenty-eight thousand personal interviews required considerable time to study and digest. Program planners are primarily interested in findings that imply alternative designs and locations for programs. Most adults (94 percent) were interested in some sort of learning, although the means of satisfying this interest varied with the individual. Middle-income adults preferred learning in traditional education settings, while adults with less than a high school diploma showed a greater tendency to favor nonschool settings such as learning at home, individual instruction, and use of community settings as learning sites.

Interests of adults also differed by age, sex, family income level, and previous education. The particular learning preferences of groups such as the educationally disadvantaged, older adults, women, and other potential participants can be described. For example, potential high school equivalency learners share special needs and characteristics that distinguish them from other adults. Generally, the strongest interest in this program is expressed by young, low-income, and minority-group adults who consider learning to be related to employment. These adults require special efforts to inform them about existing learning activities: 60 percent lacked information about local programs and nearly half had participated in no learning activity since school. Nearly 90 percent said that counseling would help them to get started, especially since over 20 percent expressed a concern about failing or not doing well (New York State Education Department, 1977).

Similar profiles can be composed for other groups of potential participants in continuing education. Although these findings aggregate responses from many adults and do not adequately portray individual needs, interests, or barriers, they describe present and potential participants. Thus they can stimulate thinking about issues that require community response.

Suggestions for Practice

Designing a needs assessment that would respond to the many information needs of planners at state, local, and community levels posed unique challenges. Because results were eventually to be used by both state and local administrators, a balance between data for general planning purposes and detailed information about learners in particular communities was required.

While the New York needs assessment has supplied a large data base for planning learning for adults, there are some dangers that may arise from interpretations of the results. Adults who respond to questions about their preferences in the delivery of services answer out of their own fund of experiences. If those surveyed have no knowledge of innovative programs or activities, they will not mention them. This tendency to choose familiar settings and techniques favors "tried-and-true" delivery methods at the expense of innovation.

In a statewide assessment, findings pertain to large projections. Frequently, attention focuses on the most popular choice or upon the typical choices of a certain group of learners. For example, the interview results picture the typical older adult learner as a person with less than a high school education and a family income of $10,000 or less. This person is motivated to learn for personal enrichment or to develop an avocation. The characteristics of adults over fifty-five are, however, diverse. Most older adults did name avocational interests, but nearly one-third of those who were still employed were interested in job-related learning, and more than one-tenth wanted to study for a diploma, license, or other certification. These totals, while not large in comparison to other choices, still represent sizable numbers of potential learners. In New York, the 1970 census figures point out that one-tenth of adults over fifty-five represents nearly 400,000 individuals. The same data could thus be used in different ways — to restrict or to expand alternative educational services.

These dangers and other issues relating to the interpretation of findings were brought to the attention of program administrators in the workshops held across the state. One of the special strengths of the study has been increased involvement of users of the results in all phases of the work. As a result, there has been a greater commitment to use of the findings in decision making. The state education department has developed and begun to implement a plan to use the information for administrative decisions and legislative recommendations. Several regional organizations use the data to assist in coordinating existing programs. Many local districts have employed survey findings to reveal alternative ways of delivering learning activities and targeting services and information to special groups of learners.

The beginnings of regional cooperation and structure have been established across the state. The efforts of educators in the field, volunteer interviewers, and others who contributed to the planning, collection, interpretation, and dissemination of the needs assessment data have resulted in an extensive data base for planning at moderate cost to local practitioners.

Translating Plans into Practice

The goal of most needs assessments conducted by program planners and administrators is to provide improved activities more responsive to those needs. The New York State continuing education needs assessment is but one example of an ever-growing series of assessment studies, illustrating some practical rules for similar research into adult learning needs.

References

Boaz, R. L. *Participation in Adult Education, Final Report, 1975.* National Center for Education Statistics, U.S. Department of Health, Education and Welfare. Washington, D.C.: U.S. Government Printing Office, 1978.
Carp, A., Peterson, R., and Roelfs, P. J. "Adult Learning Interests and Experiences." In K. P. Cross, J. Valley, and Associates (Eds.), *Planning Non-Traditional Programs: An Analysis of the Issue for Postsecondary Education.* San Francisco: Jossey-Bass, 1974.

Johnstone, J., and Rivera, R. J. *Volunteers for Learning: A Study of the Educational Pursuits of American Adults.* Chicago: Aldine, 1965.

New York State Education Department. *New York State Continuing Education Needs Assessment.* Report No. 1: Statewide Analysis. Albany: New York State Department of Education, 1977.

Tough, A. *The Adult's Learning Projects.* Toronto: Ontario Institute for Studies in Education, 1971.

Tough, A. "Major Learning Efforts: Recent Research and Future Directions." *Adult Education,* 1978, *28* (4), 250–263.

*Helen C. Veres is research associate with the Institute for Occupational
Education in the Department of Education at Cornell University.
From 1975 to 1979, she served as project director of the
New York State Continuing Education Needs Assessment.*

A comprehensive needs assessment should provide information about educational and organizational needs, settings, and methods.

Comprehensive Statewide Needs Assessment of Community College Library Personnel

Robert P. Means

During the past ten years, continuing education for librarians and library staff has received considerable attention from their national and state professional associations. Prior to this time, continuing education in librarianship typically consisted of sporadic efforts on the part of library schools, library associations, and individuals. These efforts were usually intended for a select group of librarians, mainly administrators. Most of the continuing education activities failed to provide continuity between pre-service and in-service educational opportunities for library personnel. However, with the vast growth of information, the introduction of new technology in libraries, expanded information demands from a highly educated populace, and changing library services for greater numbers and types of patrons, discussions and actions related to developing continuing education activities for library personnel at national, regional, state, and local levels have increased (Stone, 1972).

One major statewide effort was initiated by the Illinois Library Association (ILA). The ILA became increasingly aware of the need to provide leadership in the development of continuing education programs for its membership. The ILA's Committee on Continuing Education for Librarianship commissioned a study to ascertain the continuing education needs of all types of public and private community college library and learning resources center (LRC) personnel in Illinois. The study was conducted by the Office for the Study of Continuing Professional Education and the Library Research Center, University of Illinois at Urbana–Champaign (Means, 1976).

Why Community College Library Personnel?

Library and learning resource centers were developed to serve students engaged in traditional as well as nontraditional modes of study (such as programmed instruction). The development of nontraditional study materials often required that library and LRC personnel develop new skills in order to assist faculty in developing curricula that would incorporate media and instructional capabilities, including slides, cassette and video tapes, and computer-assisted instruction.

Community college library and learning resource centers represent a young, vibrant, and innovative library system not beset with the organizational, operational, and personnel constraints of more traditional systems. Libraries and learning resource centers offer traditional book and serial holdings as well as media and graphic capabilities and thus require a variety of personnel with differing educational needs. These conditions of expanded library services and related changes in traditional staff responsibilities made community college library and LRC personnel a promising clientele for continuing education.

Rationale for the Needs Assessment Approach

Several factors influenced the decision by the ILA committee on continuing educational for librarianship to conduct a comprehensive statewide needs assessment study of community college library and LRC personnel (including administrators, clerks, aides, media specialists, technicians, and graphic artists). The primary objective was to assess the educational and organizational needs of personnel. Additional information, which would assist ILA in making future decisions related to the development of continuing education activities, was also needed. These other information needs included: increased understanding of the characteristics of all types of personnel (including work experience in the library field and educational background), of personnel preferences for materials and methods used in continuing education activities, and of institutional and organizational factors encouraging or inhibiting personnel involvement in continuing education. The ILA staff anticipated that this information would be helpful in its efforts to understand and make decisions about ways of linking the educational and organizational needs of library practitioners to knowledge resources within universities (for example, to schools of library science).

Steps in Design and Implementation
of the Needs Assessment

Use of questionnaire survey techniques enabled the committee to accomplish the study objectives quickly and systematically. The content and format for the needs assessment questionnaire was developed in several phases. The basic framework was derived from a review of previous needs assessment studies of library personnel, from which categories of questions were selected. Faculty members from the University of Illinois Library Research Center served as content experts to aid in delineating the proficiency areas required of library personnel who must respond to emerging technological developments. These content areas became the focal point for identification of educational and organizational needs. The staff from the Office for the Study of Continuing Professional Education compiled questions related to contexts in which continuing education might occur and preferred educational methods or materials.

The final questionnaire used a nine-page multicolor format (colored paper was used to distinguish the questionnaire from the regular mail personnel would receive). Directors of library learning resource centers in all forty-eight community colleges were phoned and asked to participate in the study. All but two agreed. Questionnaires were then mailed to directors in accordance with the number of persons working full- or part-time as administrators, clerks, aides, media specialists, technicians, and graphic artists. Two weeks after mailing, all directors were contacted again to ensure that they had received the questionnaires and to remind them to distribute copies to staff. Respondents were each given a self-addressed stamped envelope so they could complete and return their questionnaires anonymously.

Two pilot tests were conducted during questionnaire development. Library and LRC personnel in two community colleges were asked to complete the first draft of the questionnaire. As a check on the reliability and validity of parts of the questionnaire, especialy for purposes of clarifying categories of job-related tasks, respondents were asked some of the same questions in either a follow-up personal interview of phone call. Using the results of the first pilot test, six types of library and LRC personnel were identified in terms of job-related tasks and educational and organizational needs.

A second pilot test was conducted with a sample that included the six types of personnel. Questions and categories were reviewed by phone with randomly selected respondents. The added benefit of phone calls was that individual interest regarding continuing education was heightened. In several instances the person contacted became a representative within the institution, who helped encourage others to complete the questionnaire as part of the final survey phase of the study.

The questionnaire in its final form included three major categories. Data from these categories were useful to planners of continuing education activities. These categories included:

1. *Setting:* characteristics of library personnel and the institutional and organizational units where they work;
2. *Educational needs:* inventory and ranking of needs related to continuing education activities related to specific job responsibilities; and
3. *Preferences for methods and types of continuing education:* sources of information (books, conversations with colleagues) personnel find most effective in efforts to continue their education including location, duration, and time most appropriate for scheduling these activities.

Knowledge of Setting

The questionnaire included items on characteristics of library and LRC personnel, the extent to which personnel keep abreast of changes in the field, and the incentives and obstacles within the personnel's work environment that influence participation in continuing education activities.

Background Information on Libraries and LRCs and Demographic Information on Personnel. This section of the questionnaire was designed to provide a profile of individual libraries and LRCs (for example, size of book and media collections, number of staff, population served). This information was requested only from directors of libraries and LRCs. Additional questions were asked that permitted classifying jobs, delineating age groups, and determining personnel's previous formal work experience in a library. These data served as independent and intervening variables and were used to explain differences in the educational needs of various categories of personnel.

Keeping Current in Your Field. A series of questions was asked to ascertain the type and degree of respondents' involvement in continuing education during the preceding twelve months. Respondents were asked to describe involvement within and outside their institutions in both formal degree and nondegree activities (such as professional association meetings). These data provided a means for indicating the availability of such activities within institutional settings and a measure of the library's and LRC's willingness to encourage personnel participation in continuing education.

Incentives to Participation. This section of the questionnaire was designed to elicit information regarding those factors within work settings that encouraged participation in continuing education (such as higher salary, encouragement from supervisor, having nearby opportunities for continuing education). Respondents were asked to rate incentives in terms of their relevance to determine the influence they had on their decision to participate. Respondents were also asked to rate the extent to which each incentive was currently available within their work setting.

Obstacles to Participation. To understand personal and work environment factors that affect participation in continuing education, a series of questions was designed to identify existing obstacles and the extent to which they inhibited participation (for example, demands of current job responsibilities that restrict participation, lack of encouragement from administrator or supervisor, and lack of awareness of programs available). When reviewed in conjunction with findings describing incentives to participation, these data enabled planners to identify critical constraining factors with the greatest effect on participation and enabled them to design strategies to reduce those barriers.

Knowledge of Educational Needs

To ascertain the educational needs of all levels of library and LRC personnel, a modified task analysis was devised. This section of the questionnaire, entitled "Description of Current Work Activities and Educational Needs," contained 127 brief descriptions of tasks, divided into nine categories (operation and management of libraries and LRCs, development of educational programs, instructional tasks, cataloging and classification, circulation, clerical tasks, reader services, production services, and acquisition and selection). Respondents were asked to identify major and minor tasks that they performed during a typical work week. Major tasks meant twenty percent or more of their time was devoted to the task, while minor tasks required less than that amount. Respondents then indicated each of those tasks in which they had major or minor continuing education interests. Major continuing education interests meant that respondents were willing to spend two or more full days at an educational activity (such as a workshop or seminar) sometime during the year. Minor continuing education interests meant they they were interested in reading or discussion, but not to that extent. Major and minor interest levels as defined in this study were used as indicators of educational need because they served as measures of motivation and commitment to continuing education activities. Using these ratings, needs were ranked in relation to specific categories of tasks.

One of the major strengths of this modified task analysis approach to needs assessment was the opportunity it provided to rank, compare, and contrast library and LRC personnel needs by various role perspectives (for example, administrator or graphic artist). Completion of this section of the questionnaire served as a way for personnel to audit their jobs and review the extent to which they perceived a need to improve performance through educational or organizational change related to various tasks. It also enabled continuing education planners to form a list of priority needs directly related to work tasks. This increased the chances that personnel would be motivated to participate, particularly if they perceived an opportunity to improve job performance, increase job satisfaction, and receive some rewards for doing so.

Knowledge of Preference for Methods and Types
of Continuing Education

Two types of questioning techniques were used to learn preferences for instructional formats. Respondents were asked to rate "types of materials and information used for professional development." This included lists of print materials (such as professional journals and books), nonprint materials (including cassette tapes and slides), and interpersonnel contacts (such as conversations with fellow staff) that were most effective and least effective in their professional development. The generated data were reviewed in conjunction with responses to questions about "types of continuing education activities you prefer." This included a list of combinations of formal continuing education activities (degree programs, institutes, seminars, workshops), of varying lengths of time (half-day, one semester) located in various settings (home, one's own institution, nearby college). Respondents were asked to rate whether they highly preferred an activity and would participate or would not participate. Additional questions were used to identify the months of the year and the days of the week personnel preferred to participate. Analysis of responses to both sets of questions revealed patterns in preferred methods, types, locations, and durations.

Procedures for Data Analysis

Responses were received from 262 individual library and LRC personnel, representing 54 percent of the 497 who received questionnaires and forty of the forty-six community colleges that initially agreed to complete questionnaires.

The most useful comparisons were those of educational needs of the six personnel types and of various age groups. Frequency distributions provide basic summary statistics (frequency counts, means). One-way analysis of variance identified significant variations of respondents by type or age of personnel. Subsequent comparisons (Scheffe Test) were used to decide which categories were significantly different. Discriminant analysis was used to select which educational needs, labeled "administrative" and "technical," were associated with specific personnel types and age groups.

Major Findings and Implications

The findings from the three major components of the questionnaire (setting, educational needs, and preferences for methods and types of continuing education), reviewed individually and in combination, offered valuable insights and direction for the development of continuing education in relation to the educational and organizational needs of library and LRC personnel.

Questions regarding *Knowledge of Setting* generated the following findings:

1. Descriptions of resource centers made it possible to identify both public and private libraries and LRCs with similar characteristics (such as print and nonprint collections and types of staff) and similar educational

needs. This information was helpful in indicating institutions likely to partici- pate in specific types of collaborative activities. It also defined the predomin- ant needs of various geographic locations within the state.

2. Profiles of respondents indicated that community college personnel were younger than their counterparts in other library systems (56 percent were thirty-six or younger—40 percent of the directors were included in this cate- gory). Sixty-four percent of the respondents had completed a bachelor's degree or more. Age and formal education were associated with patterns of participa- tion. The results of this study were consistent with those reported in other studies (Johnstone and Rivera, 1965; Knox, 1968).

3. Findings regarding the extent of previous participation in continu- ing education activities helped portray an environment where continuing edu- cation, particularly of a formal nature, was not very prevalent. Only 22 per- cent of the respondents had attended any in-service meeting and only 8 per- cent indicated that in-service was more than a once-a-year activity. Twenty- seven percent of the respondents (mostly administrators) reported having attended a workshop, seminar, or institute related to job or career interests in the past twelve months. Half of the respondents had engaged in a formal edu- cational activity within the past five years. These findings helped substantiate the void in continuing education opportunities available to all types of library and LRC personnel within and outside their work settings. In addition, they indicated the need to acclimate many individuals to formal learning, particu- larly those who had not recently engaged in such activities.

4. Factors within the work setting rated as having the greatest influ- ence on participation in continuing education included "increased job satisfac- tion," "accessibility to nearby opportunities for participation," and "rewards for participation" (particularly monetary rewards). However, these same items were not rated as being currently available within the work setting. "Release time," "availability of tuition rebates," and the "willingness of individuals to increase personal and professional competence as reward for participation" were available. Major "obstacles to participation" listed by personnel included: "problems getting time at or away from work to engage in continuing educa- tion," and "the money to do so," with the additional problem of "not knowing what is available." This information helped continuing education planners better understand the factors and incentives that would be most likely to influ- ence an individual's decision to participate in continuing education.

Data from a section on "knowledge of needs" were used to establish pri- orities of needs by various types of personnel (such as librarians and media specialists). Listed below is a composite of these needs related to five general task areas: (1) administration and supervision of libraries and LRCs; (2) cur- riculum development—assisting faculty in curriculum planning and produc- tion of instructional materials; (3) teaching—improving ways in which librar- ies and LRC personnel can provide training to faculty, administrators, and students regarding use of information and instructional resources of the libraries and learning resource centers; (4) technical services—improving technical aspects of acquisition, cataloging, classification, and circulation; and (5) reader services—improving general information services provided to patrons.

The results indicate needs for continuing education activities that will lead to both educational and organizational change. Five major needs were identified that continuing education could help to meet.

1. Competencies in initiating and completing administrative, management, and supervisory changes in the library and LRC operation, involving the addition of media services and learning skills center components, the acquisition of new information resources and instructional technology, and the influx of new staff.

2. Better communication among personnel to provide suggestions for short- and long-range planning of library and LRC services and increased opportunities to resolve staff problems through constructive dialogue and discussion about alternative decision-making strategies.

3. Improved understanding of the adult learner clientele. This might include a series of activities discussing the interrelated concepts of: the psychological, physiological, and socioeconomic characteristics of adults that affect learning; the educational needs and interests of adult learners; the motivation of adult learners; and types of information (resources) and delivery systems most suitable for adults.

4. Program development skills that are essential in designing learning experiences for adults, such as how educational needs are assessed, how educational objectives are developed, how to effectively utilize existing information resources and professional expertise of personnel in one's library or learning resource center, what types of alternative delivery systems can be used to conduct educational activities, and how to evaluate educational activities, including both the processes used in development and the outcomes of those activities for improving future efforts.

5. Technical skills related to introduction of new equipment and its maintenance, new systems for acquisition, cataloging, and storage, and evaluation techniques that measure the extent to which services offered by the library or LRC are cost-effective and compatible with users' needs.

Responses to the section on "preferences for methods and types of continuing education" were most informative when combined with data from the section on "setting." This combination of responses improved understanding of why certain forms of continuing education were more popular than others. While overall attendance in formal continuing education was low, other forms of continuing education were both popular and effective, including tours (exchanges) with other libraries, reading books on professional development, dialogue with peers in their work settings, and self-directed learning activities. There was a substantial interest in degree study with specific requests for the university to offer night courses as part of extension programs throughout the state. Preferences for formal continuing education included seminars, workshops, and institutes of half a day to three days, offered near the home or place of work.

Using Survey Findings

A study that compiles a large amount of data has a variety of information to disseminate to a substantial number of persons who may want to use its findings. In this case, each interested group benefited from different information and required different modes of presentation of the findings. Requests for study findings required a variety of responses. Information provided to individuals who had received a report of findings and wanted to initiate professional development programs was different from that required by the ILA Committee on Continuing Education. Preliminary findings were released to the ILA Committee on Continuing Education for Librarianship for review, reactions, and suggestions for further analysis. As results from more complete analysis became available, executive summaries were provided to participating community colleges with suggestions for next steps in designing continuing education activities. Regional meetings of the ILA and special community college library and LRC groups provided forums in which the project staff was able to disseminate findings. These sessions offered an opportunity to validate and clarify findings as well as make suggestions regarding strategies for implementing continuing education activities. Every effort was made to translate the study findings into information useful in setting up continuing education activities.

A number of persons requested information that would provide a better understanding of the needs assessment technique used in the study so the process could be modified for continued use in institutional settings. Information describing this project's needs assessment process became part of the summary statements provided to interested individuals and institutions.

Strengths and Weaknesses of the Approach

Every needs assessment technique has specific strengths and weaknesses. In this study strengths were involved in both the needs assessment approach and the implementation process. The use of a questionnaire allowed for the collection of large amounts of data in a short period of time, using a relatively inexpensive process, while maintaining respondent anonymity. The questionnaire provided a mechanism for assessing educational and organizational needs of personnel by role perspectives; helped to describe work environments (including the climate for institutional and organizational changes and respondents' learning preferences — information instrumental for planning continuing education activities), and provided a model that individuals and institutions were able to use in their own settings.

Pilot tests provided an opportunity for library and LRC personnel to participate in the design of various components of the final instrument, increasing their interest and motivation to be part of the study and influencing them to encourage colleagues to participate. The process used to develop the questionnaire and to disseminate findings provided opportunities to link library personnel in one institution with those in another; improve the state professional library association's link with regional and local membership; and increase sharing of resources between library personnel, the state professional association, and the state's universities. The needs assessment process thus served as a catalyst for individuals, institutions, and the state library association to review and take action on their priority educational needs. Dissemination of the findings provided both an opportunity to enrich the data base with respect to personnel needs and a forum in which to suggest strategies for implementation of continuing education activities.

In a comprehensive statewide needs assessment the scope of the study, data collected, results available, and number of persons wanting to use the findings increase the magnitude of problems. Several suggestions resulting from this study may assist persons in avoiding problems in planning and implementing a needs assessment.

It is essential to develop a coordination plan for a comprehensive needs assessment approach. The logistics of planning, conducting, and disseminating results from a comprehensive statewide study require extensive communication efforts that need to be carefully orchestrated. However, persons conducting needs assessments should be cautioned against using comprehensive studies to collect extensive amounts of information, much of which may not be useful, nor ever shared. Steps need to be taken to develop a clear rationale for each question to ensure that the same information is not already available from existing sources, that the respondent possesses the information desired, that the questions will elicit the data desired, and that the findings will eventually be of some benefit to the respondent. Completion of a questionnaire may raise respondents' expectations regarding the result of their efforts on continuing education offerings. If no activities are planned as a follow-up to the needs assessment study, consideration should be given to providing individuals or institutions with information about activities that are already available that they might attend. Needs assessment studies often fall short of their potential value because they fail to translate needs into educational activities which benefit the respondent — the potential participant.

References

Johnstone, J. W. C., and Rivera, R. J. *Volunteers for Learning*. Chicago: Aldine, 1965.
Knox, A. B. "Emerging Directions in Continuing Professional Education." Chicago: Consultation on Continuing Education, 1968.

Means, R. P. *A Study of the Continuing Education Interests of Illinois Community College Library Learning Resource Center Personnel.* Urbana–Champaign: Office for the Study of Continuing Professional Education, University of Illinois, 1976.

Stone, E. W. *Report of Association of American Library Schools Continuing Education Committee on Questionnaire Responses Relative to Continuing Library Education as it Exists in American Library Association Accredited Graduate Library Schools and Their Parent Institutions.* Washington, D.C.: Department of Library Science, The Catholic University of America, 1972.

Robert P. Means is assistant director, Office of Continuing Medical Education, Department of Postgraduate Medicine and Health Professions Education, University of Michigan Medical School, Ann Arbor, Michigan.

In planning a new off-campus graduate degree program for adults,
attention should be given to assessing needs
both externally and internally.

Needs Assessment in Planning Graduate Degree Programs

Linda K. Bock

This chapter describes a needs assessment strategy for assessing client interest in a graduate liberal arts degree for adults. Conducted over a three-year period to assist program planning, the needs assessment was initiated and conducted by a continuing education specialist in the Office of Continuing Education and Public Service (OCEPS) at the University of Illinois at Urbana–Champaign.

Background

The concept of a graduate liberal studies degree, the Master of Arts in Liberal Studies (MA/LS), is about twenty-five years old but has become more popular in recent years. About thirty institutions now offer MA/LS degrees. Awareness of their success led to our consideration of a MA/LS as a viable offering of the University of Illinois at Urbana–Champaign.

OCEPS staff saw an opportunity for initiating a new part-time liberal studies degree program for adults. The staff was also aware of institutional questions that needed attention before final decisions could be made by the college of liberal arts and sciences, the graduate college, the university senate, and the Illinois Board of Higher Education as to whether the university should offer a new degree program. There were three central issues:

1. Was a new degree for adults of sufficient priority within the mission of the university? (The faculty and administration needed to make this decision.)
2. Was there sufficient client and faculty interest and support for the program? Three surveys were conducted to help find out if there was client interest. Committees were formed to build faculty support. (The faculty and administration needed to make this decision.)
3. How should the program be structured to satisfy both the requirements of the institution and the needs and wants of faculty and clientele? (The clientele, faculty, and administrative staff needed to make this decision.)

The Process

To deal with each of these central issues, a small committee was formed, consisting of staff from continuing education, the college of liberal arts and sciences, and the school of humanities. Various strategies, techniques, and approaches were used to gather information for decision-making purposes regarding each of these three issues. In this process, both comparative and normative data were collected (McMahon, 1970).

One type of comparative data was information about other programs. The first step in deciding how to deal with the three central issues was to learn from successfully operating programs. This included contacting the Association of Graduate Liberal Studies Programs (AGLSP). This association was most helpful in providing "data sheets" on all member programs. These data sheets included information about number of students enrolled, occupations of students, administrative arrangements, and samples of curricula. Valuable information was acquired from the data sheets on individual programs. It was found that all programs rest on the acceptance of the concept of graduate liberal studies within the scope and central mission of the institution. Most programs are administered by the campus office for continuing education and/or the summer session office, while academic control is usually the responsibility of the academic departments and the graduate college.

Faculty advisory councils and curriculum committees are often established to oversee curriculum content and design, instruction, and evaluation. These supervisory committees generally include faculty members from throughout the liberal arts fields, some of whom are involved in the MA/LS program. However, program structure varied substantially among institutions. Some programs are designed with clear and well-defined subject matter, while others are dependent upon student and advisor initiative. Nearly all programs are designed with a particular clientele in mind. The clientele vary considerably, but it is apparent that the largest single group of all MA/LS students are secondary school teachers and others involved in education. Homemakers and persons from professional fields such as engineering, nursing, and law constitute other large segments of the clientele. Institutions draw their faculty mainly from the parent institution and professors are almost always hired on an overload basis. The majority of the programs are basically summer school or evening programs, though there is substantial variation.

After studying the characteristics of successful existing programs a "Summary of Master in Liberal Studies Program Characteristics" was prepared as the first working document in the needs assessment and program planning effort. The project staff then read annual reports, program proposals to university senates, monographs, and the general literature on external graduate degrees. This review uncovered issues about which the faculty and administration at the University would likely be concerned—including quality assurances for the program.

Other institutions were visited. Early in the process, two members of the committee visited programs at Johns Hopkins University (whose program has served as a model for most in the country) and the University of Oklahoma. The University of Oklahoma, in addition to having a distinguished program, had the advantage of being situated, like the University of Illinois, away from major population centers (Burkett and Ruggiers, 1965). These visits were very helpful in seeing successfully operating programs firsthand, as well as in providing an opportunity to question faculty, staff, and students about issues they felt were important. Brochures collected from other institutions provided detailed knowledge about their programs. This research lasted one academic year. With this background the study was expanded to include faculty members and other administrators who would be directly involved in the decision of whether to initiate a new adult degree program.

The needs assessment used three information-gathering techniques to provide background for the two faculty committees and to determine whether there was a clientele for a MA/LS program. These techniques included telephone surveys, interviews with prospective clientele, and formation of a citizens' advisory committee.

Normative data were collected both within the institution and from potential participants. Two faculty committees discussed the proposed program for several years. The task of the first-year senior faculty committee was to study the desirability and feasibility of a university graduate liberal studies program for adults in light of the mission and resources of the campus. During the year, the initial small needs assessment committee shared findings with the faculty committee. A statewide survey was then conducted to ascertain potential student interest. The result of this phase of the study was affirmative and the first-year committee recommended that a new faculty committee be appointed the following year to design the MA/LS program.

The statewide survey was designed to gather general information concerning preferred topic areas as well as preferred scheduling, locations, and methods of instruction. The sample of respondents consisted of adults throughout the state who were identified by the University of Illinois regional program directors (field staff) as representative of those who would have an interest in a MA/LS program. Each person was sent a letter about the proposed program, followed by a telephone interview conducted by members of the regional staff.

Seventy-three persons were interviewed by telephone. Thirty-one communities throughout the state were represented. Several occupational and other groups were represented. Those groups served by similar programs elsewhere showed the highest potential interest in a MA/LS degree program (professionals, homemakers, engineers, businessmen, military personnel, and educators). Senior citizens were also included in the sample.

The following year, as faculty exploration progressed, two similar surveys were conducted in the same way — a letter followed by a phone interview — in two pilot areas. The purpose of these surveys was to obtain information about topic interest and scheduling. The findings among the three surveys were similar, yet distinct enough to warrant a separate survey in each pilot area.

In all three surveys, small samples were taken (seventy-three persons statewide: thirty-five in one pilot area and fifty-eight in the other). In each survey persons were identified who were likely to have an interest in graduate liberal education — in some cases the individuals were known to the interviewer. Clearly, these surveys were not representative of the total adult population. They were designed to provide a sense of the market rather than a firm prediction of behavior. Nowlen (1980) points out, "The commitment of time, money, and attention provides a much firmer basis for predicting future enrollments by similar adults than checking a topic on an interest inventory. This approach is disadvantageous when information from a needs assessment is required to plan a sample program."

Survey Results

The survey findings were very useful. Between 58 and 65 percent of those interviewed indicated they would very likely enroll in a graduate MA/LS program. The types of adults most interested in the program were professionals, educators, homemakers, and businesspersons. This was similar to the clientele in similar programs nationwide. The age span of adults most likely to enroll was thirty-five to fifty years. Topics of particular interest were studies of foreign cultures, literature, fine arts, contemporary issues, sociology, and psychology. Preferred scheduling was weekday evenings from 7–9 P.M., twice a month. There was interest in a one- or two-week summer session on campus. In addition to the telephone surveys, several personal interviews were conducted to probe deeper than the telephone survey: these interviews yielded no important additional information about schedules and subject matter interests, which convinced the committee that the telephone survey had served its purpose. The personal interviews were enlightening, however, in revealing an intense concern of potential clientele for program quality.

Those respondents who showed the most interest and excitement about the program were asked to be members of a citizens' advisory committee. Approximately twelve to fifteen persons in each pilot area were asked to serve. Two citizens' advisory committees met during the year with the second faculty committee that was designing the degree to participate in an exchange of views of the program. They will continue to be involved as a sounding board before important final program and scheduling decisions are made. They will also assist in marketing the program by identifying organizations and groups to contact and by reacting to publicity plans.

As planning progressed, information was obtained from conversations with consultants and from participation in workshops. The director of graduate liberal studies at Johns Hopkins University and the dean of the college of liberal studies at the University of Oklahoma were invited to campus for two days of consulting with the faculty committee planning the program. The consultants' visits were helpful in many ways, particularly in encouraging the committee to continue with the program design that was taking shape.

Several members of the faculty committee attended a workshop on humanities continuing education sponsored by the National Endowment for the Humanities and the National University Extension Association. In addition to sessions devoted to descriptions of successful programs already funded, the conference allowed the committee team an opportunity to work on the MA/LS project and to consult with interested persons. As a result of that consultation, the committee was encouraged to send a preliminary proposal for a development grant to the National Endowment for the Humanities, and did so.

Assessing Faculty Interest

The project staff sought to assess potential faculty interest, while at the same time informing departmental executive officers about the program and exploring with them possible administrative arrangements for faculty participation in the program. Meetings were held with departmental executive officers and selected faculty members from the School of Humanities and the School of Social Sciences. At those meetings various committee members explained the MA/LS concept, described the developing program design, and responded to questions. Despite some wariness about the potential cost of the program, most faculty members and administrators who took part in those meetings approved the MA/LS concept and expressed a desire for some form of participation by faculty from their units.

Suggestions for Practice

A strength of the exhaustive process used was that the faculty members and administrators who planned the program felt that they had an opportunity to study the idea thoroughly and contribute to the program. Information was also available describing what the prospective clientele felt was important to them, though this kind of client input is not foolproof, since people were responding to an idea and not a program. The weakness of the needs assessment process was the length of time (three years) it took to complete. Part of the reason for this extended length lay in the nature of the sponsoring institution and the extensive process necessary for the consideration of new degree programs, but another reason may have been that the study was overly thorough.

The first step in initiating a graduate liberal studies program should be to contact officers of the Association of Graduate Liberal Studies Program. They will be able to suggest people to contact in similar institutions. By telephone conversations or by visiting a similar institution, much basic information can be quickly and easily gained. The most essential factor is finding out the specific preferences of the target group, followed by educating faculty about the program and promoting it to them.

References

Association of Graduate Liberal Studies Program. *Statement of Purpose*. Middleton, Conn.: Wesleyan University, n.d.

Burkett, J. E., and Ruggiers, P. G. *Bachelor of Liberal Studies: Development of Curriculum at the University of Oklahoma*. Boston, Mass.: Center for the Study of Liberal Education for Adults, Boston University, available from Syracuse University, Publications in Continuing Education, 1965.

McMahon, E. E. *Needs of People and Their Communities and the Adult Educator*. Washington, D.C.: Adult Education Association of the U.S.A., 1970.

Nowlen, P. M. "Origins." In *Developing, Administering, and Evaluating Adult Education*. San Francisco: Jossey-Bass, 1980.

Linda K. Bock is a continuing education specialist and coordinator of community education at the University of Illinois at Urbana–Champaign. She is the author of Teaching Adults in Continuing Education, *a monograph for new teachers of adult students.*

Programs for educationally underprivileged persons will succeed to the extent that participants learn to assess their own needs on a continuing basis.

Needs Assessment for the Educationally Underprivileged

Beverly B. Cassara

Needs assessment is an integral part of the process of education. The developing ability of learners to assess their own educational needs on a continuing basis throughout life will determine the quality and amount of lifelong learning. This is equally true for the more educated person and for the educationally underprivileged. Persons with much education are most likely to seek more. It would seem that better-educated persons have somehow learned to assess their own needs, whether they do this formally or informally, consciously or unconsciously. If the concept of lifelong learning is to be implemented, a curriculum must be developed that teaches the youngest learners how to begin assessing their own needs and how to continuously develop both short- and long-term goals. Goal setting and needs assessment have always been implicit in the process of education and deficiencies cannot be quickly corrected in educational programs for undereducated adults. Attempts to provide instant solutions through education and skill development can do a disservice to the educationally underprivileged.

Whose Needs?

The term *needs assessment* means different things to different people. This chapter is concerned with ways of developing individuals' abilities to assess their own learning needs. Society has needs, too, needs that have to be assessed and fulfilled by adults in learning situations. Society has a need to help the poor become self-sufficient. This need must be addressed in terms of problems, resources, and goals. Those who are conducting needs assessments for the educationally underprivileged should clearly conceptualize whose needs are being addressed and realize that in the case of the individual, while some initial assessment is called for, real assessment will go hand-in-hand with the ongoing learning situation. There are different levels and purposes for needs assessments. The needs assessment of a community, no matter how small, tells us little about the individual learning needs of the educationally underprivileged person.

Which needs should have priority? Situational factors will dictate much of the answer. Therefore, it is important that individual adults be directly involved in assessing their own needs and that the individuals decide whether those needs can be met through a continuing education program. This is especially true for persons whose lifestyles are unique because of their cultural backgrounds or for the educationally underprivileged. Any other path is disrespectful to them and may undermine the educational efforts they are making on their own behalf.

A Case Study—Working with the Tenants of a Housing Project

It is no coincidence that many poorly educated persons end up in housing projects and remain wards of society even though the city may provide many kinds of opportunities for adults to improve their education. Why do these persons not take advantage of the learning activities afforded them? Over a five-year period, students in a course entitled "Educational Problems of Mature Women" at Federal City College (now the University of the District of Columbia) and a number of volunteers went into a housing project to study this problem. It was a small study in one 155-unit housing project, but it yielded significant findings. At the time of the initial survey there were twenty-six male heads of households. Most families had at least five children, many had ten, and a few had up to seventeen. Many, though not all, of the families were on welfare.

The women in the housing project were not ignorant or unintelligent; in fact, many were sophisticated in dealing with life in modern urban America. What they lacked was organized knowledge and specific skills. Therefore, they did not have the credentials important to enter the mainstream. Formerly, most either accepted their second-class citizenship resentfully or apathetically. Many were hopeless and cynical and did not believe that there was a way to break out, not even through education. With the various movements toward equality in the past two decades and the influence of the mass media, expectations are now being raised. The second-class citizenship syndrome is not quite the steel trap it used to be. Now more continuing education programs are based on the important precept that adults should become autonomous learners who decide what, where, and why they need to learn.

The education committee of the tenants' association of this housing project invited the students and volunteers to work with them. They wanted to improve their opportunities but did not know how to go about it. The initial dialogue developed over time into a small educational center at the housing project. The women were willing to help get needed information, but they were adamant that they did not want to become simply objects of a study. They felt that if we cared enough to want to find out about them, then we must come to work with them and help them as respected and equal fellow human beings, who want to be masters of their own fate. The challenge to work with them to solve their problems was accepted.

Assessing Needs—A Continuing Process

There are several things to be said in favor of unfunded programs. In the first place, anyone who works in such a program has to have some intrinsic motivation. Secondly, without funds one cannot immediately set up an elaborate program, only to discover flaws after the fact. Finally, there is no pressure to perform against an arbitrary deadline.

To start, there was an initial needs assessment survey. The assessment group teamed up with members of the community to go door-to-door on a Sunday afternoon. A questionnaire was used to solicit demographic information as well as information about the educational interests of those we interviewed. Only after some months into the project did the assessors learn that educational needs solicited in this manner have little or no relation to reality. In the first place, persons approached in this way do not have a considered opinion on the tip of their tongues as to what their educational needs might be. It takes more than one short interview to even begin to elicit from them their best ideas about their needs. In the second place, people have many motivations for giving the answers they do, such as a desire to sound impressive, or a quick answer to get rid of the intruder, or some impractical flight of fancy.

With results from these data the school was in no position to float a number of courses immediately—which was just as well. An initial group of ten to fifteen interested women sat down to discuss the results of the survey and to explore next steps. It was realized that for the moment what they wanted more than courses was the opportunity to sit around the table with the interesting university students and carry on a dialogue with them in an informal way. There was no point in trying to start any formal classes until the women were ready. If they did not know what they really wanted, they knew what they did not want.

These dialogues continued for some months. The women wanted particular community leaders to come in as speakers. They wanted to see films about black history. Also, they asked for job counseling and placement information. The class provided these services to them. Certain students took on the special problems of individual women and went back to the project several times a week to follow up on particular matters. It was not, however, until nearly a year had passed that the women were finally reassessing their own needs and deciding that they were ready for more formal learning. They seemed to come to the conclusion that the university students were successful because they had studied formally and that there is no shortcut to success. They dreaded going back to pick up junior high and high school subjects. When they finally decided it was time to start Adult Basic Education (ABE) and General Educational Development (GED) work, some small classes were established using the makeshift facilities of the recreation room, the rental office, or the office of a social service agency located on the premises. The university students were the teachers.

But it did not quite work that way, or not for long. It became apparent that it is difficult to work with these women as a group because each is at a different level of educational achievement, and some would not work in a group because they were too proud to show what they did not know. Therefore, as a next step, the women were divided into groups of two or three. Some were given individual tutoring. Ten of the women were making definite progress toward the GED exam. The group as a whole also continued to meet from time to time, especially to discuss money-making projects to pay the cost of the GED exam, babysitting, and other issues.

During the entire process, the women were being encouraged to consider what education is for, what it is worth, what difference it could make in their lives, and to explore various means to set realistic short-term goals, as well as to continually assess their own needs in order to make progress toward achieving these goals. When the first two women passed the GED, the expectation of entering college had developed. The staff began advising the women on admission procedures, financial aid possibilities, and courses of study.

At one point, the facilities seemed too small. There was a desire to accommodate more women by moving to a local public school as an evening program. Although it was only two and one-half blocks from the project, a number of the regulars dropped out. Others from the larger community joined the group, but there was tremendous pressure on us to come back to the project, which we finally did.

The reasons for the attitude of the project women should not be taken lightly. They included (1) the pride of having the center in their project; (2) the need to be on the premises, where their children were nearby at home; (3) physical problems or fatigue after a tiring day that made it difficult to get to the school; (4) the fact that we had to keep raising money to pay the required fee of a janitor each night we used the building; and (5) their reluctance to go to their children's school, even if it was for adults and in the evening.

Of the subjects that the women requested, some failed and some succeeded. One that failed was furniture refinishing. There seemed to be quite an interest in this subject. When the class was unsuccessful the first time, it was tried again under other circumstances with a different teacher, but it soon petered out. In assessing their needs and discussing why this happened, the women concluded that materials cost more than they had realized; it was lonely work, each in her own house, when they would rather be involved in the comings and goings of the community; and after it was accomplished, a refinished piece of furniture would make no real improvement in their lives. The learning that occurred as these women identified their own needs was worth the effort. Learning from failure is a natural human way to learn. The women did not need to be saved from their failure. They learned some important things about themselves. They were able to reassess their needs in terms of new knowledge.

During the years of working with these women there were a number of surprises. Who would have guessed that after cooking for large families all day, the women would want to study cooking? They had never really said so, but when various foods were brought in by the college students for refreshments, the women were curious about how they were made. One night when they asked me how I made some rolls, I realized that showing would be better than telling, so we spent an evening making rolls. After that the students often cooked the refreshments on the premises and those interested participated— but all enjoyed the eating.

The need for social reinforcement was very strong through the first years of the program and social occasions were part of the ongoing program. Later, after several of the women went off to college, the women gradually became more independent of the group and more self-sufficient. However, they did maintain a loyal supportive relationship, studying together for exams and sharing babysitting and transportation as much as possible.

The women began to realize that there were many tasks they could perform for themselves that they had previously thought impossible. They recognized that instruction in peer counseling could help them in their daily community life. After six weeks of study in this subject one morning each week, each woman chose a special counseling project, which was carried out under the supervision and guidance of the study group. Through this course, new knowledge about themselves led to reassessment of educational as well as other needs.

When the women asked for driver education, there was some concern about the appropriateness of this subject for the women who could not afford cars. This concern came from persons who were being asked to support this activity through funding and who tended to reply that proposals were not economically feasible. They thought they knew what the women needed better than the women themselves. The funding sources did not consider what having a driver's license could do for these women. Finally, driver education was provided by some driver education teachers in the adult education master's program, who got credit for it as their practicum requirement. Driver education was very successful. Why? The women needed the driver's license for identification and it served as a tangible symbol of self-respect. Also, in many cases friends had cars they could use for shopping in better markets outside their community. They gained self-confidence by seeing that they could drive as well as other people.

In program planning for the educationally deprived person, needs assessment is an ongoing, dynamic process. It is the basis for program planning, which in its turn should be flexible enough to provide opportunities for gaining new knowledge as it is needed. The teacher, program planner, and counselor should be sensitive to the development of the participants. The participants should be seen as whole persons and educated as whole persons, taking into account all their problems, interests, concerns, special abilities, and cognitive learning styles. Educational deprivation has affected all aspects of their lives and the remediation must do so, too. A woman who meets the challenge of getting a driver's license may have the confidence to conquer mathematics. A woman who took peer counseling in order to help her neighbor eventually took a master's degree in counseling.

Persons of limited knowledge and experience need to reassess their needs and goals often as their intellectual horizons expand. "The hope of helping the educationally underprivileged lies in catering to those needs which they themselves recognize as urgent and in using flexible informal teaching methods" (Lowe, 1975, p. 30).

Defining Success

It is the most natural thing in the world for continuing education practitioners to want to define success and judge adult learners against the definition. There are institutional constraints that force us to try that approach. Institutions are held accountable for the dollars they receive, and in traditional situations students have to be graded. While it is gratifying to know that fourteen of these women entered college and two will be graduating next semester, we cannot use this as a yardstick. Just as some women do not wish to learn to type, others do not want to go to college. We could look to the fact that two of the women at least have been able to improve their job situations and earnings so that they have been able to move out of the project. However, all do not have the desire to move out of the project. Therefore, the best evaluation is self-evaluation. Personal self-evaluation must be built into the learning process. Without it, one cannot reassess needs or set goals.

Consider the lot of some women in this housing development. They are most likely to be single heads of households. They have slim prospects of ever becoming economically self-sufficient. They have no career aspirations to give purpose to their lives. They have little prospect of having a caring mate with whom to share their later years. Their living situation leaves much to be desired. Often they have accepted the second-class status projected onto them and they do not even like themselves. Sometimes their large families are due to their lack of knowledge of alternatives, but often they are intentional. Producing children is one of the most wonderful things in life and they can share equally in that. This gives them a family to absorb their strength and energy. It gives them problems, to be sure, great and unsolvable problems, but in a sense gives them a career. Educational remediation cannot be achieved through quick training or one-shot educational ventures. To help persons whose lives have been so scarred, it is necessary that teacher, counselor, and trainer have patience and perseverance.

"Don't come to study us. Come to help us as friend to friend." Adult education practitioners who realize that education is truly a lifelong process will not be so concerned about getting everyone at some magic cognitive threshold but instead will cherish the possibilities of continuing dynamics.

Reference

Lowe, J. *The Education of Adults: A World Perspective.* Paris: UNESCO Press, 1975.

Beverly B. Cassara is the dean of graduate studies and a professor of adult education at the University of the District of Columbia.

At least 50 percent of requests to develop new training might be
eliminated or redirected if a systematic approach
to needs assessment were employed.

A Systems Approach

Judith Fidler
David R. Loughran

In this era of rapid technological change, continuing education is assuming an increasingly important role in the industrial setting. This role reflects a growing awareness of the effectiveness of continuing education in overcoming performance problems and associated costs of developing sophisticated training programs and educational systems to solve these problems. In response to these developments, the British Columbia Telephone Company adopted General Telephone and Electric Service Corporation's program design model, *A Systematic Approach to Curriculum Development* (1976), which relies heavily on what is probably the most important, yet most frequently neglected, step in industrial education — the front end, or needs assessment. This chapter describes this process as it is conducted within the British Columbia Telephone Company (B.C. Tel) and illustrates its practical applications.

The Needs Assessment Process

In B.C. Tel the needs assessment process is conducted to ensure that valuable educational resources are deployed to design and deliver educational programs only when education is a reasonable solution in overcoming a performance discrepancy. Problems may be identified by any member of the organization. They are generally brought to the attention of the company's education center in the form of a written request to design a new course. This request initiates the needs assessment process, which is conducted by continuing education specialists. The needs assessment process is divided into three major phases: (1) identification and quantification of all symptoms of the problem and definition of the performance discrepancy, which is a description of the difference between what employees are doing and what they should be doing; (2) classification of the problem in terms of its probable cause or causes, based on three categories: a lack of skills or knowledge, an environmental or procedural condition, and a motivation or incentive condition; and (3) generation of alternate solutions to the problem: this phase includes the identification of associated costs and benefits and results in a recommendation to implement the most reasonable solution.

Identification, Quantification, and Definition

Identification, quantification, and definition are the initial three steps in conducting a needs assessment. When a request to design an educational program is received by a training specialist, it is generally written in broad, nonspecific terms that describe a situation or perceived problem from the perspective of those people who are affected. These broad statements are sometimes useful as goal statements but have limited value in defining specific performance deficiencies. It is the responsibility of the continuing education specialist to meet with the originator of the request to attempt to rewrite these goal statements in terms of specific, observable performances. This step is called *identification*. It is also sometimes referred to as *goal analysis*. The resulting rewrite will reflect the performance problems to be overcome and must be stated in terms that are acceptable to all concerned.

Once this step has been accomplished the parameters and guidelines for the balance of the needs assessment are established and stipulated in a written contract. The contract includes answers to such questions as:

- Will the educational specialist be permitted to investigate problems in supervisor job performance if they appear to be related to the performance problems of the staff?
- Will the educational specialist be permitted to work with members of support groups in the interest of evaluating the efficiency and clarity of existing performance objectives or standards?
- In analyzing job performance, will the educational specialist be permitted to interview job incumbents while they are performing their duties?
- Will the educational specialist be permitted to interview job incumbents at all, or will the specialist have access only to the supervisory staff?

With these guidelines established, the educational specialist can proceed with the next two steps, quantification and definition.

In the quantification step, the educational specialist determines the magnitude of the performance problem by obtaining information on the types and numbers of employees affected and the frequency of errors that result from the problem. In this way, the specialist can decide how important removal of the problem is to the overall operation.

In the definition step, the educational specialist defines the performance discrepancy in terms of what employees are doing compared to what they should be doing, according to the operating standards for the job. This ensures that everyone concerned with the problem has a clear understanding of it and that solutions will be oriented to eliminating specific performance discrepancies. This step is critical to needs assessment. Without a precise definition of the performance discrepancy, further analysis to identify causes of the problem or to generate solutions is impossible. Once the problem is defined, the second phase of the needs assessment, classification, is conducted.

Classification

In this phase, the performance discrepancy is further analyzed to identify its probable causes. Mager and Pipe, in *Analyzing Performance Problems* (1971), suggest three classifications for performance discrepancies, which are used in the *Systematic Approach to Curriculum Development* model:

1. Skills Discrepancy. (The employee is not performing to standard because he doesn't know how or he cannot perform because he has never been taught or because he has forgotten.)
2. Environmental Discrepancy. (The employee knows how to perform and is motivated to do so, but something in the work environment is preventing him or her from doing the job correctly — such as lack of or poor quality tools or absence of adequate performance procedures and standards.)
3. Motivation/Incentive Discrepancy. (The employee knows how to do the job, has the skills to do it, but for some reason does not want to do it.)

Classification of the performance discrepancy in this way focuses on causes of the discrepancy rather than on its effects. It also identifies those problems involving proficiency discrepancies that can be solved by education. This ensures that the limited resources of the education center are used only when education represents a viable solution.

Alternate Solutions

In this phase, the educational specialist reviews all the data collected to this point and generates a number of possible solutions to the problem. Each potential solution is analyzed to decide which is the most cost-beneficial to the organization. The result will be the substance of the specialist's recommendations.

The contract document drawn up in the identification step outlines the method (written, oral, or both) of making the final recommendations and identifies the individual to whom the recommendations will be given. The final report consists of five parts: (1) An introduction that states the goals of the analysis and outlines any previous work that relates to those goals; (2) A method section that defines the population that took part in the analysis and the procedures of the needs analysis; (3) A results section that reports the specialist's findings, which is often broken down into parts, discussing each step of the analysis separately; (4) A discussion section that explains the findings and identifies the limitations of the analysis, based on the original contract document; and (5) a recommenations section that contains the specialist's recommendations, as well as associated costs and benefits to the organization.

Because the needs assessment process and the educational specialist role is a new one, not yet fully understood by some managers who see continuing education personnel primarily as instructors, the recommendation step can test the specialist's diplomatic skills. This is particularly true when the analysis does not result in the recommendation of education, but focuses on nontraining areas of the organization. Approval of the final recommendation goes far to enhance the acceptance of both the needs assessment process and of the educational specialist role within the organization.

Application of the Needs Assessment

The following describes how the needs assessment process was applied to a perceived educational problem in B.C. Tel. This particular problem was identified by a continuing education manager in the company's education center, whose department was encountering difficulties conducting effective needs assessments.

There are ten training departments in B.C. Tel, each serving a different functional discipline within the organization. In each department, certain educators specialize in program design. All program designers take a two-week course in the *Systematic Approach to Curriculum Development* (1976), in which they learn to use the standard company systems approach. A centralized curriculum development and evaluation group, reporting to the director of training, delivers this course, provides assistance to the program designers, and evaluates their work. This provides consistency and ensures that the company standards for program design are maintained.

The problem identified by the education manager was that his education specialists were not being accepted by the line organization when they attempted to conduct needs assessments. He requested the development of a new program to teach his employees to become more effective in dealing with line personnel. This request was directed to a member of the curriculum development and evaluation group, who met with the education manager to conduct the first step of the needs assessment process.

Identification. During the interview with the education manager the request for education was reworded to identify the following more specific, observable problems: on two occasions in the previous six months line managers had refused program designers access to their areas to conduct a needs assessment; the line managers had stated that needs assessment disrupted their operations and they the purpose of the educators in their offices was not clear; and program designers themselves felt inadequately prepared in methods of collecting data for needs assessment.

Quantification. At the present time there are fifty employees prepared in program design who could be faced with the task of conducting a needs assessment. Staff turnover in this area is estimated to be about 10 percent a year and the curriculum development and evaluation group prepares about twenty new program designers for the education departments each year. If the company standard is properly administered, a needs assessment should be conducted for every request received to develop a new educational program. On a company-wide basis, such education requests are generated at a rate of about fifteen to twenty each month.

Definition. The actual performance of program designers was compared to the standards defined in the *Systematic Approach to Curriculum Development* and discrepancies were defined in the following areas: program designers were not using standard interview techniques, questionnaire design methods, or group techniques to collect data for needs assessment; and program designers were not establishing a written contract to define the scope of the analysis, describe the data-collection methods to be used, and provide guidelines for reporting recommendations.

Classification. The causes of these performance problems were classified as skills discrepancies, environmental discrepancies, and motivation/incentive discrepancies. Although program designers accepted the importance of needs assessment and understood the steps in the process, they had never been taught to apply basic data-collection techniques in conducting needs assessment. Clearly, program designers were not using correct interview techniques, questionnaire-design methods, or group data-collection techniques, because they had never received preparation in these areas. This problem was caused by a lack of proficiency.

Despite the existence of a recognized policy regarding the necessity of written contracts for needs assessment, program designers were not writing them. The causes of this discrepancy were classified as both envirronmental and motivation/incentive. The condition was considered to be environmental because the policy did not include documented guidelines for the program designers' reference when writing contracts. The discrepancy was also classified as motivation/incentive, because the education managers were not insisting on the establishment of written contracts for every needs assessment.

Alternate Solutions. It was proposed that the skills discrepancy could be addressed in three ways:

1. Improve the resources available to course designers on data collection techniques by augmenting the education center library. Because of the limited nature of such resources, the cost of this solution was estimated to be no more than $300.

2. Design an educational program for course designers to provide the proficiency required to use basic data-collection techniques. The estimated cost for such a program was $10,000.

3. Purchase an off-the-shelf educational program in data-collection techniques. The cost of the available courses ranged from $3,000 to $18,000.

It was suggested that the environmental discrepancy could be eliminated by either or both of the following solutions: writing a procedural document to describe the content and format of a contract for education (the approximate cost of this solution was estimated at $300); and designing a two-part form to be used as a training contract for education (the approximate cost for the design of the form and a two-year supply was estimated at $1,500).

To solve the motivation/incentive discrepancy, the following remedies were considered: advising education managers that they must review all training contracts for education with their course designers before the quantification step is initiated; and making the curriculum development and evaluation group responsible for coordinating the needs assessment process and for ensuring that contracts are established consistently. The costs associated with these remedies were considered negligible.

Another solution to all three problems would have been simply to ignore them. However, based on records from the Bell System Center in Illinois (Svenson, 1978), the consistent application of needs assessment to requests for education reduces the number of educational programs developed by roughly 50 percent annually. In B.C. Tel, this factor alone would account for a minimum annual saving of $900,000. It was recommended that the skills discrepancy be overcome by purchasing additional resource material on data-collection techniques for the education center library and designing an in-house educational program on data-collection techniques, which seemed more cost-effective than purchasing an off-the-shelf program, as internal design would ensure that specific needs were met.

To overcome the environmental discrepancy, it was recommended that a procedural document be drafted to describe the content and format of contracts for educators. Designing a two-part contract form was eliminated as being too restrictive.

Finally, to solve the motivation/incentive discrepancy it was suggested that the curriculum development and evaluation group assume responsibility for coordinating the needs assessment process. It was felt that this would ensure that contracts were written in a consistent manner.

These recommendations were made to the education manager who initiated the request. They were accepted as viable means of overcoming the problems his program designers were having in dealing with line managers when conducting needs assessment.

Conclusions and Implications

The needs assessment process has proven to be a powerful tool in analyzing performance problems and making cost-effective recommendations regarding continuing education. Despite the fact that it can be a time-consuming process, the benefits it offers far outweigh the alternative of developing needless educational programs. However, certain difficulties in applying the process cannot be overlooked: (1) the role of the educational specialist in conducting needs assessment is a new one, which has not yet been accepted by many managers outside the organization; (2) the process may appear threatening to some managers because it may disclose problems that cannot be overcome through an educational effort; and (3) cost-benefit analysis is difficult to conduct because most industries do not have a data base related to the cost-effectiveness of education. Nonetheless, a systematic needs assessment process, such as the one described in this chapter, allows educational departments to focus their resources on the design and implementation of education to solve specific performance problems, to increase their effectiveness, and to account for their costs.

References

General Telephone and Electronics Service Corporation. *A Systematic Approach to Curriculum Development.* Stamford, Conn.: General Telephone and Electronics Service Corporation, 1976.

Mager, R. F., and Pipe, P. *Analyzing Performance Problems.* Belmont, Calif: Fearon Press, 1971.

Svenson, R. A. "Strategic and Current Planning for Technical Management Training." Madison, Wisc.: American Society for Training and Development, 1978.

Judith Fidler is employed in the curriculum development and evaluation group at British Columbia Telephone's education center in Vancouver, British Columbia.

David R. Loughran is education coordinator, curriculum development and evaluation, for the British Columbia Telephone Company.

*For an evaluation of the feasibility of a new graduate program
that would serve many part-time students, needs assessment
required analysis of potential participants, the university,
faculty, competing programs, and potential employers.*

Assessing the Need
for a University Program

Linda K. Gunzberger

Deciding on a needs assessment procedure in higher education requires consideration of several issues. At Loyola University of Chicago a needs assessment procedure was used to decide whether to establish a master's degree program in public administration that would serve many part-time students.

In recent years the graduate school office and other offices in the university have received numerous inquiries for information about a program that would prepare graduates for administrative positions in public agencies. To decide whether Loyola should offer a public administration program, the dean of the graduate school appointed an interdisciplinary advisory committee to assess needs, a well-known approach (Hospital Continuing Education Project of the Hospital Research and Educational Trust, 1970). The committee members represented the political science department, the institute of industrial relations, the medical school, and the school of social work — units which had received inquiries about a public administration program. The dean of the school of business was consulted as a resource. A graduate assistant helped with administrative details.

Following the emphasis on objectives stressed by Mager and Pipe (1962), the committee first defined what should be known about a master's in

The contents of this chapter reflect the work of fellow committee members Melvin Dubick, Kathleen McCourt, Alan Fredian, and Marla Goodman.

public administration degree program. The committee members decided on the following tasks: to define a public administration program, to identify other programs both nationally and locally, to obtain information about students' needs from potential employers, to document philosophy, to identify curriculum, and to make recommendations.

Defining the Problem

When the committee first approached the question of a master's program, there was no agreement whether such a program should be developed or what it should be called. It was agreed that a master's program should prepare students in the administration of federal and state agencies, local governments, community organizations, or health care institutions, and it was decided that "master's degree in public administration" (M.P.A.) was an appropriate designation.

Identifying Other Programs

Knox (1979) argues that examination of other programs can suggest ideas about educational needs. Although inquiries regarding a master's in public administration were documented by the graduate school office and a poll of faculty members revealed support for a master's degree program that would prepare graduates for administrative positions in public agencies, it was decided to research similar programs, both nationally and locally. It is possible that the level of interest expressed by the students and faculty was a reflection of other programs and an additional program might not be successful. Three questions were asked: (1) What is the significance of the M.P.A. nationally? (2) What is the nature of the competitive programs? and (3) Can Loyola provide a distinctive program?

National Programs. In recent years, there has been a growth of public sector agencies in the United States. One result of this growth is the need for effective, well-prepared administrators. The National Association of Schools of Public Affairs and Administration (NASOAA) has 215 members. Data were gathered from these institutions concerning M.P.A. programs' content, core areas, and emphases. From this data, it was clear that the programs in the Chicago area reflected the national scope of M.P.A. programs. There were six such programs in the immediate Chicago area, as well as comparable programs elsewhere in the state.

Local Programs. After reviewing each of the local programs, summaries were drafted that indicated their major characteristics and distinctive features. Comparisons of the administrative structures and instructional components of these graduate programs provided a comprehensive view of what is currently available at other institutions in the region and made it easier to identify the unique contributions that a new program at Loyola could make.

Determining Students' Needs

Knowles (1978) contends that society's perceptions of desired performance obtained from research and experts' reports provides one means of assessing needs. The proposed M.P.A. was intended for students from the Chicago area. Most potential participants would hold or aspire to managerial positions. The program could provide both in-service education for those already in careers and preservice education for those seeking to begin careers in public administration. A letter from the City of Chicago director of personnel and a letter from the assistant to the mayor of Chicago for manpower indicated the availability of support for the program and of tuition reimbursements for students.

A market survey was conducted that had three purposes: to examine the need for another M.P.A. program in the area, to receive comments and suggestions for the curriculum, and to estimate potential participation in the program by those surveyed (taking into account tuition reimbursement or internship sponsors). A key to this needs assessment was recognizing what a learner needs to learn and how best to serve those needs (Knox, 1977). A letter addressing those issues was sent to local government officials, community organization leaders, and health care officials. All communities within a one-hour drive of each university campus were contacted by letter. The survey results were as follows:

Local Government. The best response was from local government officials, to whom sixty-nine letters were sent. Thirty-one responses, including twenty-five letters and six telephone calls, were received, representing a 45 percent response. Fifty-eight percent of the respondents said that they believed that there is a need for the proposed M.P.A. program and 23 percent said there was not. Some of those who responded that there was not a need for a general M.P.A. program expressed their support for individual courses in public administration, in such areas as labor relations, land use and zoning, and public finance and budgeting. Nineteen percent said they they did not know whether there was a need or market for the proposed M.P.A. program. Responses of local government officials indicated that:

- Enrollment of local government employees in work-related courses is encouraged and the tuition reimbursement incentive would be universally offered to those wishing to enroll in our proposed program.
- Many of the respondents would be willing to serve as sponsors in the practicum phase of the program, including both those who then supervised internships and those who did not.
- The need for proficient administrators in such areas as municipal government, public finance and budgeting, and building and land use (planning and zoning) was continually stressed. Other areas mentioned included administrative law, interpersonal skills, and electronic data processing.

- Even respondents who indicated a lack of need for a generalized M.P.A. expressed approval of the curriculum and wished to be informed of developments in the implementation of a Loyola M.P.A. program.

Community Organizations. Leaders of Chicago-area community organizations were contacted, as the committee had originally considered a community organization administration track as an area of concentration within the M.P.A. curriculum. In this case, however, the response was poor. Of twenty-two letters sent, only two responses were received. Due to the poor response, the proposed track was eliminated.

Health Care Officials. Public health care officials were surveyed to ascertain the need for a proposed public health and hospital administration track. Again, as with community organizations, the response was not encouraging. Most respondents were partial to the master of public health degree, as opposed to a specialized health track within an M.P.A. program.

Responses to this survey were valuable to this committee for purposes of curriculum development. Although it was decided not to implement the community and health tracks at this time, suggestions made in those areas have been noted for possible future use. Through the use of this survey, numerous valuable contacts were made. The respondents to the survey are to be kept informed of Loyola M.P.A. program developments.

Documenting Philosophy

There are a number of factors that can combine to give Loyola a distinctive new program, one that should attract students and establish itself in the Chicago area. This is important, because a needs assessment should include an internal assessment to be sure that identified needs are met. Loyola's existing programs and departments provide the university with a foundation for the M.P.A. program. Various departments that were contacted expressed a willingness to cooperate. They constituted resources for an interdepartmental M.P.A. program. Additionally, Loyola is a university committed to the city. Knowledge of the processes and problems of cities is an essential ingredient in training professional public administrators. Finally, Loyola is a religious institution with a long tradition of emphasizing the value and ethical components of education. Today more than ever, ethical questions are likely to be complex. The proposed M.P.A. could include courses that concern themselves directly with value confrontations and ethical decisions that confront administrators. Given national and local trends, it was decided that the proposed M.P.A. program can attract students to Loyola and enhance the reputation and vitality of the university's graduate program.

A primary issue in most of the early committee discussions was whether there is sufficient demand for another M.P.A. program in this geographic area. Responses fom surveyed public managers indicated the potential demand for the proposed curriculum, as well as an interest by their employees.

Many of the local programs suffer from too many or too few restrictions on student enrollment. A program at one institutions is highly selective (and quite costly for many potential enrollees), while another M.P.A. program admits most applicants. With these points in mind, Loyola's program is designed to be accessible, but also maintains a reasonable standard for admission, one that fits into the university's overall objective of quality education. Loyola also has a location advantage. With three strategically placed campuses, Loyola provides excellent locations in the Loop, north of the city, and south of the city. A third advantage is a specialized M.P.A. program. Many other programs in the area are management curricula which have been adjusted to public sector needs. They are built onto a business school or management school and do not reflect the needs of government sector students. The proposed M.P.A. program is structured as a separate degree program under the graduate dean and is intended to serve students wishing to enter or already working in public administration.

Based on the committee's inquiry it was proposed that Loyola University of Chicago establish an "Institute for Public Administration and Policy." The central components of this program are techniques for evaluating programs, analyses of problems, economic institutions, social policy, and research skills.

References

Hospital Research and Education Trust. *Training and Continuing Education.* Hospital Continuing Education Project of the Hospital Research and Educational Trust. Chicago: Hospital Research and Education Trust, 1970.

Knowles, M. *The Adult Learner: A Neglected Species.* (2nd ed.) Houston, Tex.: Gulf, 1978.

Knox, A. B. *Adult Development and Learning: A Handbook on Individual Growth and Competence in the Adult Years for Education and the Helping Professions.* San Francisco: Jossey-Bass, 1979.

Mager, R., and Pipe, P. *Analyzing Performance Problems.* Belmont, Calif.: Fearon Press, 1972.

*Linda K. Gunzburger established the office of postgraduate medical
education at the University of Chicago and designed the
division of continuing medical education at Loyola
University of Chicago. She is also a consultant
to the Association of American Medical Colleges
for continuing education and evaluation.*

Procedures for developing a diabetes educational profile to assess the educational needs of patients with a chronic illness can help others in constructing similar instruments.

Diagnosing the Educational Needs of the Chronically Ill

Wayne K. Davis
Alan L. Hull
Michele L. Boutagh

Living with a chronic health disorder requires the active involvement of patient and family in the therapeutic program. To prepare diabetic patients and their families to assume some responsibility for their own health care, individualized and comprehensive education is required. This education should be aimed at increasing the patient's understanding of the disorder and its treatment. In many cases, it also requires a change in attitude and performance on the part of the patients and their families.

The need for patient education based on a complete educational diagnosis (needs assessment) is clear. A committee of the American Public Health Association reported: "An essential component of health care is the education

This project was supported by a contract with the Michigan Department of Public Health, division of chronic disease control. Information about obtaining copies of the Diabetes Educational Profile for needs assessment purposes can be obtained from Wayne K. Davis.

of the patient. To achieve optimum results an educational plan should be developed . . . and should be reassessed periodically since the patient's educational needs change depending on such factors as his medical condition, his knowledge, attitudes and abilities" (American Public Health Association, 1972, pp. 6-7).

A significant problem in the education and care of the diabetic patient is the lack of adequate information about the patient's educational needs. While health providers are experienced in the diagnosis of physical needs, they are not expert in assessing educational needs. Therefore, many health care providers prescribe educational interventions without knowledge of the patient's health behaviors and attitudes, the amount of information the patient has already acquired about the disorder, the family situation, or other relevant factors. This lack of information about the patient makes it difficult for health professionals to provide appropriate and meaningful education. Moreover, many health professionals do not take full advantage of available interactions with their patients to effectively communicate information or to instill the desire and capability to carry out the treatment plan.

Several researchers have examined the practitioner-patient interaction and its effect on patient learning and subsequent behavior (Becker and Maiman, 1975; Davis, 1966, 1968; Hulka and others, 1975; Korsch, Gozzi, and Francis, 1968; Podell, 1975; Svarstad, 1976). These studies have focused on the traditional setting where an interviewing process is used to elicit information. A consistent finding is that practitioners' perceptions about the extent of patient knowledge and self-management differ markedly from actual measures of these variables. Based on a review of the compliance literature and empirical testing, Davis (1966) concluded that physicians are usually unable to predict which of their patients will be noncompliant or to identify patient characteristics that may point to noncompliance.

To increase the usefulness of the provider-patient interaction and to facilitate the process of data collection, many nurses and dieticians have developed assessment instruments for their own purposes. In an activity related to the current project, over 200 different diabetes patient assessment forms were collected (Boutagh, Hull, and Simonds, 1979). Most of these instruments were limited in scope and did not assess factors known from prior research to be indicators of educational needs. Typically, these instruments have been developed to meet the needs of an individual hospital and data are not available regarding their reliability or validity. There is a need for a carefully developed, reliable, valid, and comprehensive diabetes educational profile (DEP) to assess the educational needs of diabetic patients. This chapter describes the development of such a DEP. The basic steps in the process are applicable to the preparation of most needs assessment instruments.

The first step in the development of the diabetes educational profile (DEP) was to define the universe of items that, in prior research and clinical experience, have been important in the diagnosis of educational needs. Three activities yielded the preliminary list of patient characteristics to be considered for inclusion in the diagnostic instrument. A literature review was conducted that included approximately 250 relevant articles (literature that described factors that influenced educational outcomes). From this review, a list of over 500 potentially important characteristics was generated. In-depth interviews with physicians, nurses, dieticians, diabetic patients, and family members were used to add variables to the list. These interviews confirmed the relative importance of the variables identified through the literature search. There was much overlap in what the diabetic family member and health provider groups thought was important to assess. Nonetheless, the value of feedback from these different perspectives was evident. For example, the health professionals often stressed information related to the patient's capability and willingness to comply. Diabetics and their family members, on the other hand, emphasized psychosocial data, such as their emotional reactions to diabetes and the degree of stress in their lives. The list was then reduced and refined by removing items judged by the health providers to be relatively unimportant, and by combining redundant items. The result of this reduction was a list of 144 characteristics.

A questionnaire was developed, based on this list of patient characteristics. The 144-item questionnaire was mailed to 1,518 individuals, including the entire membership of the American Association of Diabetes Educators (AADE) and a representative sample of 300 Michigan nurses selected from visiting nurse and public health agencies. The initial questionnaire was mailed in September, 1978. In October a follow-up reminder was sent to those who had not returned the questionnaire.

The survey recipients were asked to evaluate the relative importance of each of the 144 items on a seven-point scale, ranging from (1) "not at all important" to (7) "very important." After they had responded to each of the items, they were asked to circle the ten most important items.

There were two purposes in the analysis of the returned questionnaires: to reduce the number of characteristics to a manageable subset of items that would be included in the first draft of the DEP instrument, and to ascertain the conceptual structure of the items. In reducing the number of items, the relative importance of each was considered as well as its relationship to other items. Mean ratings and frequency of selection as one of the ten most important characteristics were used to identify the items considered most important by the respondents. Factor analysis and cluster analysis techniques were employed to arrive at an empirical grouping of items on the basis of their interrelationships.

Results

Of the 1,518 questionnaires mailed to potential respondents, 802 completed questionnaires were received by the cutoff date. Six hundred sixty-nine

(83 percent) were received from members of AADE and 133 (17 percent) from Michigan nurses. Although most respondents rated all items on the questionnaire, returned forms that had more than eight unrated items were not included in the final analysis. Descriptive statistics were computed for each item.

The average rating for all items was 5.64 (standard deviation = .15). The items were rank-ordered by mean rating and by the number of times the item was judged to be one of the "ten most important." Thirty-six items were removed from further analysis at this point for one of two reasons: either they had been circled as one of the ten most important items by less than seventeen respondents (seventeen was selected as an apparent breaking point, based on the distribution) or they were rated more than one standard deviation below the average rating of all items.

To arrive at an empirically determined conceptual grouping of the items, several factor analyses were computed. The result was the identification of three factors, subsequently named "demographic," "cognitive," and "psychosocial" factors. Fourteen items that were either redundant with other items or not rated as being important by the respondents and which did not load heavily on any single factor were removed from the list of items to be measured by the DEP.

The correlations among the three sets of factor scores were substantial (see Table 1). Because the items were rated by the respondents according to the importance of the specific patient characteristic, the negative correlation between the demographic and psychosocial factors and the negative correlation between the demographic and cognitive factors indicate that respondents who gave high ratings to demographic items tended to give lower ratings to the cognitive and psychosocial items.

Cluster analysis techniques were employed to identify related items within each factor. After these clusters were identified, the individual items within each cluster were ranked by the mean importance indicated by the respondents. Criteria were developed to further reduce the number of items. Based on these criteria, items were deleted when the items had relatively low mean ratings from the respondents, the information was available on the patient chart, and the information was not detailed enough to allow a specific patient care intervention.

The result of the factor analysis and cluster analysis was a list of patient characteristics which were considered by the survey respondents to be relevant

Table 1. Factor Score Correlations

	Psychosocial	Cognitive	Demographic
Psychosocial	—	—	—
Cognitive	.5501	—	—
Demographic	– .6595	– .4538	—

to the health provider's diagnosis of the diabetic patient's educational needs. These items were incorporated into a pilot instrument.

In the demographic factor the components used in the instrument were learning disabilities and frequency and content of meals. In the cognitive factor the components were understanding of diabetes (pathophysiology, etiology), blood sugar regulation, urine testing, insulin, diet, exercise, health habits, and complications. In the psychosocial factor, the components were health beliefs (including patients' perceptions about the severity of diabetes and the efficacy of the diabetic regimen), attitudes toward illness, attitudes toward health providers, compliance, locus of control, readiness to learn about diabetes (interest in diabetes education), stress, adjustment to illness, and social support.

The pilot instrument was composed of 176 items and required approximately sixty minutes to complete. Because this amount of time was deemed excessive, two techniques were used to further refine the instrument. First, three expert consultants examined the instrument and made revisions that reduced overlap and more sharply focused the content of the items. Then the pilot instrument was pilot tested in Michigan hospitals by 200 patients with diabetes.

The data generated from the test included: (1) reactions of the nurses who used the instrument regarding its validity and utility, (2) observing the patients while they completed the instrument, which pinpointed confusing or unclear questions, (3) patient responses, which were correlated to identify redundant items, and (4) indications of changes in educational interventions based on the results of the DEP use. These data were the basis for the final revision of the instrument prior to widespread use with diabetic patients.

Discussion

The multistage process described in this chapter has been successfully used in the development of an educational needs assessment instrument for patients with diabetes. The basic procedures are not unique to the current application, but can be used in the development of instruments to diagnose educational needs of patients with other health disorders. The steps for developing a needs assessment instrument could also be adjusted for use outside the health field.

The first step in the process was a meticulous review of the research literature to identify variables relevant to needs that might predict positive patient outcomes. This literature review was aimed at detecting variables that in previous research studies had proven to be related to improvement of patient education and compliance.

The second step in the process involved conducting structured interviews with diabetic patients, family members, and health professionals who care for patients with diabetes. The interviews were based on the results of the literature review. Their purpose was to elaborate and refine the variables detected in the literature.

A questionnaire was then designed based upon the literature and the interviews. The questionnaire was completed by a wide range of health professionals who care for and educate the target patient population. This third step of the process obtained the opinions of experienced health professionals regarding the relative importance of each variable. Following the return of the questionnaires, the data were analyzed regarding the reliability and the factor structure of the instrument.

Refining the preliminary draft of the needs assessment instrument was the fourth step. This time-consuming activity was probably the single most important aspect of instrument development. The translation of variables thought to be important in diagnosing educational need into actual questions that could be answered by patients was completed by an interdisciplinary team of individuals, including those with medical, nursing, public health, and educational expertise.

Pilot testing of the instrument was the fifth step of the multistage process. Patient data were collected, interviews were conducted with practitioners who used the instrument, observations were made of patients while they were completing the form, and evidence was collected regarding changes in educational interventions based upon the completed patient instrument. The results of the pilot tests allowed for final revision of the instrument.

In addition to the steps in instrument development mentioned above, numerous psychometric analyses were conducted to ascertain the factor structure, along with the reliability and validity of the needs assessment instrument. The process used to compute the instrument's validity is the multitrait, multimethod approach outlined by Campbell and Fiske (1959). The responses indicating the importance of individual items revealed that there are three major types of information used by health providers in deciding on successful educational interventions for diabetic patients: cognitive, psychosocial, and demographic characteristics.

The multitrait, multimethod process involves collecting information on several patients' traits using several different methods. Seventeen of the items in the DEP instrument were selected as the traits to be studied. Three alternative methods were used for ascertaining the presence or absence of the traits in a patient. The first method used to assess the trait was the item which existed in the DEP instrument. The second method involved restructuring the way in which the trait was assessed and including that as an additional DEP item. The third method utilized a completely different assessment method, and consisted of a questionnaire which was administered to either a close friend, a nurse, or a member of the diabetic patient's family who knew the patient well. These data were collected for approximately 200 patients and the data were coded and entered into a computer program that allowed project staff to estimate the DEP instrument's validity and reliability. The resulting instrument is now available for continuing education practitioners who want to use it for needs assessment studies.

The process followed to develop the DEP was complex and time-consuming. There were several issues faced by the staff which had to be answered during the DEP's development. One issue germane to developing any needs assessment instrument is the question of what data to collect. The staff who developed the DEP chose to ask a large number of health professionals to indicate what educational characteristics they felt were important in developing educational interventions for their diabetic patients. There are other techniques useful in' the selection of the data about educational needs to be collected (Kucha, 1974). They include (1) the individual professional, (2) a committee process, or (3) a specially formed group of experts. Frequently, individual nurses, dieticians, or other health professionals develop an assessment instrument for their own use. Sometimes these instruments are adaptations of currently available questionnaires and sometimes there are multiple instruments used in the same institution by various disciplines. Occasionally, representatives from various disciplines will collaborate within a committee setting to develop an instrument to be used in their institution. These instruments consist of items judged important by local health professionals. For example, in two projects (Etzwiler, 1973; Marquis and Ware, 1978) small groups of prominent experts in the field of health care or health education were assembled. A delphi process (Delbecq and others, 1975) was used to develop lists of patient characteristics to consider when planning educational interventions.

References

American Public Health Association. *A Model for Planning Patient Education: An Essential Component of Health Care.* Public Health Education Section, Committee on Education Tasks in Chronic Illness, Washington, D.C.: 1972.

Becker, M. H., and Maiman, L. "Sociobehavioral Determinants of Compliance with Health and Medical Care Recommendations." *Medical Care,* 1975, *13,* 10-24.

Boutagh, M. L., Hull, A. L., and Simonds, S. K. "An Examination of Current Diabetes Education Assessment Instruments." Paper presented at annual meeting of American Diabetes Association, Los Angeles, 1979.

Campbell, D. T., and Fiske, D. W. "Convergent and Discriminant Validation by the Multitrait-Multimethod Matrix." *Psychological Bulletin,* 1959, *56,* 81-105.

Davis, M. S. "Variations in Patients' Compliance with Doctors' Orders: Analysis of Congruence Between Survey Responses and Results of Empirical Investigations." *Journal of Medical Education,* 1966, *41,* 1037-1048.

Davis, M. S. "Variations in Patients' Compliance with Doctors' Advice: An Empirical Analysis of Patterns of Communication." *American Journal of Public Health,* 1968, *58,* 274-289.

Delbecq, A. L., and others. *Group Techniques for Program Planning: A Guide to Nominal Group and Delphi Processes.* Glenview, Ill.: Scott, Foresman, 1975.

Etzwiler, D. D. *Education and Management of the Patient with Diabetes Mellitus.* Elkart, Ind.: Ames, 1973.

Hulka, B. S., and others. "Doctor Patient Communication." *Journal of Community Health,* 1975, *1,* 13-27.

Korsch, E. M., Gozzi, E. K., and Francis, V. "Gaps in Doctor-Patient Communication." *Pediatrics,* 1968, *42,* 855-871.

Kucha, D. "The Health Education of Patients: Assessing Their Needs." *Supervisor Nurse,* 1974, *5,* 26–35.

Marquis, K. H., and Ware, J. E. *Behavior, Knowledge, and Attitude Variables Judged Important in Compliance with Diabetic Treatment Regimens: A Working Note for the Department of Health, Education and Welfare.* Santa Monica, Calif.: Rand Corporation, 1978.

Podell, R. N. *Physician's Guide to Compliance in Hypertension.* Rahway, N.J.: Merck, 1975.

Svarstad, B. "Physician-Patient Communication and Patient Conformity with Medical Advice." In D. Mechanic (Ed.), *Growth of Bureaucratic Medicine.* New York: Wiley, 1976.

Wayne K. Davis is associate professor and director of the Office of Education Resources and Research; Alan L. Hull is an instructor; and Michelle L. Boutagh is a program associate.

The three authors have their appointments in the department of postgraduate medicine and health professions education at the University of Michigan Medical School, Ann Arbor.
The Diabetes Educational Profile Project discussed in this chapter was funded by the Michigan State Department of Public Health.

Operational considerations can guide the development and influence the effectiveness of needs assessment studies.

Components of a Major Needs Assessment Study

Carolyn Watanabe Barbulesco

Continuing education needs assessments are usually modest efforts to identify underserved adults and estimate enrollments for proposed course offerings. Sometimes, however, continuing education practitioners want to conduct a major needs assessment study. In such instances attention to systematic procedures is especially important. This chapter reviews the operational steps in conducting a major needs assessment study. Questions that should be raised in examining operational considerations in educational needs assessment include:

- Who should be involved in the needs assessment process? To what extent is it desirable for continuing educators, clients, content or process experts, leaders in the community, lay citizens, and others to be involved in assessing educational needs?
- When in the educational program development process should needs assessments be conducted?
- How should needs assessments be conducted? What are some sources of information on educational needs? Which techniques for needs assessment are most useful? What criteria can be used to develop sound needs assessment procedures?

Who Should Be Involved in the Needs Assessment Process? Needs assessments do not depend solely on the educator to ascertain the educational needs of their clients. The client — whether an individual, members of a group, or representatives of an institution or community — should recognize the existence of the needs (Atwood, 1973; Atwood and Ellis, 1973; Knox, 1969). A more collaborative approach is required by continuing educators to assure themselves and potential participants that the client's needs can be met by the agency's program and services. Kempfer (1955) and Knox (1969) emphasize the necessity for the continuing educator to understand the importance of and develop proficiencies in bringing adult learners into the process of identifying their own needs and interests.

The voluntary nature of most educational programs for adults creates unique problems for the continuing educator. In continuing education individuals make the judgment about their own needs and what will satisfy those needs (Knowles, 1970; McMahon, 1970). Adult learners vote with their feet about the relative effectiveness, relevance, and utility of educational programs. Educational programs must be perceived by the participants to be directly related to their needs.

It is, therefore, helpful to gather data from potential participants as well as others who are knowledgeable about that client's needs (Dutton, 1970). An adult learner's willingness to engage in a particular educational activity demonstrates some personal need. Others can illuminate the magnitude and components of the identified problem.

When Needs Assessments Should Be Conducted. Needs assessments should be conducted in two situations: as an early step in planning a new educational program, or as a part of program evaluation for an ongoing educational program. In the former instance, a needs assessment is conducted to ascertain the adequacy of available programs in meeting particular educational needs and the desirability of developing a new program. In the latter case, a needs assessment can help modify an existing program to increase its effectiveness, refocus its objectives, or change the content areas by finding out how well needs are being met by the program. Because educational needs are dynamic, it is important to assess them periodically.

How Needs Assessments Should Be Conducted. Most continuing education practitioners and writers about needs assessment believe that needs ought to be the major basis for planning educational programs (Coffing and Hutchinson, 1974). Thus, how to obtain useful information about educational needs is a continual problem for educational decision makers.

Although many techniques related to needs assessments are being tried, including (1) informally asking instructors and educational administrators what they think the client's needs are, (2) formally developing questionnaires and other instruments to survey educators, community leaders, and clients, and (3) gathering empirical learner performance data through testing, there is still much to be done in the conceptualization of needs assessment procedures. It would be inappropriate to list hard-and-fast rules for conducting a needs assessment study because procedures are too new and constantly evolving.

Several sources of information about educational needs can be tapped in a needs assessment study. Some are direct sources, such as individuals or groups who can express or identify educational needs. These may include potential participants, educators, advisory groups, representatives from employers, and individual citizens. Others are indirect sources or indicators of educational needs that program planners can examine or analyze to infer educational needs. These include response level to current programs, test results, census data, mass media, professional publications, and the physical and social ecology of the community.

A major part of a needs assessment study is gathering information that identifies educational needs of potential participants. A variety of procedures or techniques can be used to identify educational needs. In some instances, educators do so on the basis of their recent experience. In other cases, educators collect new data as a basis for identifying needs. The data may involve observation, questionnaires, checklists, interviews, and inspection of documents (Campbell and Markle, 1968). Basically, needs assessment data-gathering techniques fall into two very broad categories. The first involves collecting data about educational needs from (1) needers or those who know of potential needers; (2) spokespersons for potential needers, or groups representing needers, such as representative boards (Houle, 1960), task forces (Brooks, 1972), and community leaders; (3) personnel or representatives from service agencies or other organizations who have contact with persons in need; and (4) experts (Bradshaw, 1974) with knowledge and experience in problem areas related to needers. The second group of techniques depends on inferring what the needs are through (1) observing and listening to potential needers; (2) keeping systematic records of requests for educational programs or services from potential needers or their representatives; (3) testing for deficiencies of potential needers; (4) analyzing background information as a potential indicator of educational needs of the community to be served (this information includes such aspects as population trends, history of the community, economic life, power structure, value systems, social stratification, politics and government, intergroup relations, health, and other census data), analyzing information about agencies, institutions, and services, as well as information about spatial and temporal relations of people; and (5) comparing needs with the services and programs offered to meet those needs in similar communities.

Needs assessment data-gathering techniques vary along three interrelated continuums, including the extent to which the educator or needs assessor initiates a systematic needs assessment study, the extent to which the needs assessor engages in direct communication with clients or potential clients, and the extent to which the needs assessor bases the identification and prioritization of educational needs on empirical data.

In a major needs assessment study, the process is typically defined as formal and systematic, involving at best a comprehensive examination of needs from a variety of role perspectives. Some techniques used in practice, however, are hardly formalized, systematic, or comprehensive in nature. These less systematic or comprehensive techniques include relying on hunches of experienced program planners to identify educational needs, advertising current program offerings and inferring need based on level of response, and waiting for requests from groups or individuals as an indication of need.

More formal techniques generally involve a greater degree of structure and more long-range planning. Although somewhat more structured, these particular techniques do not involve a great deal of face-to-face contact or interaction between the needs assessor and the persons or groups with the needs. These techniques include analyzing reports, publications and records, which either summarize other needs studies or provide statistical or other data that can serve as indicators of need; relying upon external consultants who are called into a situation to make an assessment of needs, based on their perceptions, expertise, and experience; observing client needs, which can range from very informal observations to highly structured and sophisticated observational research, and analyzing results of tests and examinations.

Comprehensive procedures for assessing needs, which may be combined with informal and formal techniques, include establishing and using various groups, such as advisory committees and task forces, to assist in the needs assessment; surveying clients, service providers, experts, lay citizens, community leaders, representatives of employers, and others through written questionnaires, door-to-door or telephone survey instruments, and personal interviews; and developing and utilizing systems or networks of contacts with organizational personnel to provide information about client needs by acting as a liaison between the organization and the continuing education provider.

Most of the needs assessment literature describes data sources and alternative techniques for gathering information about educational needs and concerns. Few writers, however, discuss actual techniques for analyzing needs information and for assessing or prioritizing specific educational needs. These writers (Dell, 1974; Eastmond, 1969; Grabowski, 1975; Heinkel, 1973; Knowles, 1970; Knox, 1974) suggest that once data have been gathered, they should be classified and validated for accuracy before being analyzed. The simplest and most common method of classification consists of writing each concern on a three-by-five card and then sorting these according to content area. These concerns must be organized into categories of need, which must then be analyzed to decide which are needs that can be appropriately addressed through education.

Eastmond (1969) suggests that a stated concern is a need to which an agency should respond only if it meets the following criteria. It must: show a difference between what is and what ought to be, be in harmony with the operational philosophy of the assessing agency or institution, describe a solution rather than express an unmet need or unresolved problem, and reveal a real need rather than some symptom or eccentric notion. After a concern has been deemed a need relevant to an agency, the next task is to estimate the extent of that need.

The possibility of meeting particular needs should be appraised. In making this judgment, it is important to consider several factors, such as costs, practicality, acceptability, and administrative feasibility, that might contribute to the desirable result (Eastmond, 1969; Knowles, 1970). Finally, the relative importance of the needs that have been identified should be established. If data have been gathered from a variety of perspectives, comparisons can be made among needs as perceived by educators, actual or potential participants, other representatives, or leading citizens of the community (Heinkel, 1973).

In summary, once data have been gathered in a needs assessment, several data-analysis steps should occur, including classification of the data into need areas, establishment of the nature and extent of needs, appraisal of the feasibility of meeting particular needs, and validation of needs by taking into account varying perspectives.

General Steps for Major Needs Assessments

Deciding to Conduct a Needs Assessment. This includes the recognition of a general need or problem situation and the decision to use a needs assessment study as a means to explore the desirability of a continuing education program (Copeland, 1972; Kaufman, 1972).

Arranging for Coordination of the Needs Assessment. This involves appointing an individual or group to coordinate the needs assessment study. A committee may be comprised of a representation of staff, community, administration, and clients (Cromer, 1968; New Jersey, 1974; Ohio, 1974; Rhode Island, 1975).

Specifying the Purpose of the Needs Assessment. This consists of deciding the "why" of needs assessment (Grabowski, 1975; Rookey, 1975; Witkin, 1975). It attempts to familiarize team members with the process and goal of the needs assessment (Cromer, 1968; Grabowski, 1975; New Jersey, 1974; Ohio, 1974; Rookey, 1975).

Defining the Scope of the Needs Assessment. This involves the specification of the extent of the study, whose needs are to be assessed, who should be involved in the process, and who should use the information. Management of the process, including time, tasks, resources, and talent, should be planned along with cost estimates and time lines (Cromer, 1968; English and Kaufman, 1975; Grabowski, 1975; Kaufman, 1972; Londoner, 1967; Rookey, 1975; Watts, 1974; Witkin, 1975).

Assessing Obstacles and Restraints. This consists of consideration of factors that may affect the project. These may include political or economic factors, as well as those that are internal to the needs assessment study itself (Grabowski, 1975; Rookey, 1975).

Informing and Involving the Community. It is important to create support for the study and an awareness of intended uses of needs assessment information and the kinds of administrative and instrumental decisions that will be made with the data. It is also important to indicate how various individuals and groups will contribute to the process. If people know what is happening, and how data will be used, they are more likely to be supportive (Cromer, 1968; English and Kaufman, 1975; Rhode Island, 1975; Rookey, 1975; Watts, 1974).

Identifying Symptoms of Broad Need Areas. This step identifies areas in which possible needs may exist. Symptoms are interpreted as "apparent difficulties" (Kaufman, 1972; Londoner, 1967).

Identifying and Selecting Appropriate Needs Assessment Techniques. This consists of selecting specific strategies to use in the needs assessment study. It answers the questions "What specifically are you going to do?" "In what sequence?" and "When?" (English and Kaufman, 1975; Grabowski, 1975; Kaufman, 1972; Rhode Island, 1975; Witkin, 1975).

Setting Criteria for Measuring Need. This includes setting standards related to level of knowledge or quality of skills and attitudes that are desired, against which current knowledge, skills, and attitudes can be measured (Copeland, 1972; English and Kaufman, 1975; Kaufman, 1972; Ohio, 1974).

Gathering Needs Data. This entails collecting data to ascertain the existing condition or extent of needs (Copeland, 1972; Cromer, 1968; Kaufman, 1972; Ohio, 1974; Rhode Island, 1975; Rookey, 1975; Witkin, 1975).

Summarizing the Needs Data. This includes compiling and summarizing the information gathered in the data-collection process (Cromer, 1968; English and Kaufman, 1975).

Interpreting the Data and Identifying the Needs. This phase involves comparing actual status with desired or required status, including analysis, interpretation, and evaluation of the information gathered in the study (Copeland, 1972; Cromer, 1968; English and Kaufman, 1975; Grabowski, 1975; Kaufman, 1972; Londoner, 1967; Ohio, 1974; Witkin, 1975).

Ranking Identified Needs. This is the decision-making phase of the study, in which priorities are assigned to particular needs. Decisions are made regarding which needs are most critical as well as which needs should be addressed for short- and long-range planning (Copeland, 1972; English and Kaufman, 1975; Kaufman, 1972; Ohio, 1974; Rookey, 1975; Witkin, 1975). These conclusions are usually combined with information about agency purposes and resources in the objective setting process.

Evaluating the Study. This is not essential, but if included, it occurs throughout the needs study. The questions to be answered are "Will you monitor and measure along the way?" "How will you use new information for continued improvement of the program?" and "How will you know that you have accomplished what you set out to do?" The information collected and the decisions made should be compared with the objectives of the needs assessment (Grabowski, 1975; Kaufman, 1972; Witkin, 1975).

Reporting to the Decision Makers. This step involves the dissemination of findings from the needs assessment study to concerned individuals in a form that is useful to them (Witkin, 1975).

Implementing the Findings. This is the action step, in which new course offerings, course alterations, or other adjustments are implemented. It is where the needs assessment cycle ends and begins again (Cromer, 1968).

Criteria for an Effective Needs Assessment Model

Investment of valuable resources in a major needs assessment study calls for a systematic approach. The literature suggests eleven criteria that can constitute a useful checklist for evaluating a plan for a major needs assessment study:

1. Is the needs assessment designed to identify critical educational needs and make useful recommendations to planners and decision makers? One obvious requirement of a needs assessment study is that it should yield a list of major educational needs and should provide recommendations for action to decision makers. Needs assessment should divide global needs into manageable units in order to draw effectively on the most appropriate resources (State Educational Needs Assessment Project, 1970). The study should identify learner needs and indicate some method to meet those needs (New Jersey, 1974).

2. Does the needs assessment relate to a long-range comprehensive plan? If the study ends after the needs assessment phase, there should be a way to proceed from identifying needs to the remainder of program development (Grabowski, 1975; New Jersey, 1974). The needs assessment should be designed for long-range use. From the outset, the continuing education practitioner should sell the idea that needs assessment is a long-range program (State Educational Needs Assessment Project, 1970).

3. Is the procedure simple and easily administered? It should not be complicated or require extensive training of personnel. The process should allow for convenience of respondents and elicit clear and unambiguous responses. It should be adjustable and self-correctable (Eastmond, 1969; State Educational Needs Assessment Project, 1970).

4. Is the cost for implementing the needs assessment reasonable? Costs should be limited to materials, supplies, and provisions for meetings and technical assistance. Cost of staff time can vary greatly. In some studies considerable staff time must be committed to the project; in others, very little. Although the costs of implementing the study may be minimal, the results — new educational programs or policies — may well require a major monetary commitment (New Jersey, 1974).

5. Are opportunities provided for various groups and individuals to become involved in the needs assessment process? Because of the communication demands of needs assessment, it is advisable to establish a broad base of

participation of individuals from inside and outside of education (Cromer, 1968; Eastmond, 1969; New Jersey, 1974; Ohio, 1974; State Educational Needs Assessment Project, 1970). Needs assessment studies might include professional educators; past, present, and potential participants; and members of the community (Ohio, 1974; New Jersey, 1974; SENAP, 1970). The data gathered should be as learner-oriented as possible (State Educational Needs Assessment Project, 1970). Broad participation is effective both in accurately assessing educational needs and in building public relations for an agency. Respondents should feel that their opinions are important, respected, and will be useful in the needs assessment process. The needs assessment should be adaptable to the specific situation as well as replicable in similar settings (State Educational Needs Assessment Project, 1970).

6. Are data-gathering instruments appropriate and comprehensive? Instruments should be simple, yet comprehensive enough to gather all pertinent information from appropriate sources. In addition, instruments should be field-tested for relevance and adequacy prior to use in the needs assessment study (Eastmond, 1969; New Jersey, 1974).

7. Is it clear what kinds of data are being sought? Some writers recommend that the information collected in the needs assessment process should reflect needs in the cognitive, psychomotor, and affective domains (Ohio, 1974; State Educational Needs Assessment Project, 1970). Both objective and subjective data should be collected in order to define needs accurately.

8. Does the needs assessment model provide for validity and reliability of the instruments? Effective studies require that provision be made for ascertaining the reliability and validity of instruments used to collect information about needs (Eastmond, 1969; State Educational Needs Assessment Project, 1970).

9. Does the procedure provide a method or criterion by which identified needs can be ranked? Effective needs assessments should specify a method of assigning priorities or determining the importance of identified needs (Ohio, 1974; State Educational Needs Assessment Project, 1970).

10. Has the procedure taken into account needs assessed in similar settings as well as previous needs studies conducted in the same setting? Indicating similarity of critical educational needs in one setting to those in another increases the credibility of findings.

11. Does the procedure provide for some positive initial action to address needs identified in the study? An effective needs assessment should include an attempt to initiate or revise educational programs to meet the assessed needs, so that there is some sense of action or something worthwhile being done (State Educational Needs Assessment Project, 1970).

A needs assessment study, even if carefully developed, may not adequately meet all of these criteria. There may not be full agreement on the effectiveness of a particular plan or on the value of the activities it prescribes. Nonetheless, these criteria can serve as guidelines for developing and implementing a needs assessment that will ensure that resulting educational programs will better meet the needs of clients to be served.

References

Atwood, H. M. "Diagnostic Procedure in Adult Education." *Viewpoints, Bulletin of the School of Education,* Indiana University, 1973, *49* (5).

Atwood, H. M., and Ellis, J. "Concept of Need: An Analysis for Adult Education." *Viewpoints, Bulletin of the School of Education,* Indiana University, 1973, *49* (5), 7–16.

Bradshaw, J. "The Concept of Social Need." *Ekistics,* 1974, *220,* 184–187.

Brooks, G. S. "The Task Force Approach of Determining Community Needs." *Adult Leadership,* 1972, *21* (4), 114–116, 143–144.

Campbell, V., and Markle, D. G. *Identifying and Formulating Educational Problems, Final Report.* Berkeley, Calif.: Far West Laboratories for Education Research and Development, 1968.

Coffing, R. T., and Hutchinson, T. E. "Needs Analysis Methodology: A Prescriptive Set of Rules and Procedures for Identifying, Defining, and Measuring Needs." Paper presented at American Educational Research Association annual meeting, Chicago, April 1, 1974. (ERIC document ED 095 654.)

Copeland, H. G. "Need Appraisal." Unpublished mimeographed essay. Minneapolis: Adult Education Department, University of Minnesota, 1972.

Cromer, C. A. *Procedures for Determining Vocational Education Needs Through Community Analysis.* Lincoln, Neb.: Nebraska Occupational Needs Research Coordinating Unit, Department of Health, Education and Welfare, 1968. (ERIC document ED 023 916.)

Dell, D. L. "Magnitude Estimation Scaling in Needs Assessment." Paper presented at annual meeting of the American Education Research Association, Chicago, April 1974.

Dutton, D. "Should the Clientele Be Involved in the Program Planning?" *Adult Leadership,* 1970, *19,* 181–182.

Eastmond, J. N. *Needs Assessment: Winnowing Expressed Concerns for Critical Needs.* Salt Lake City: Utah State Board of Education, 1969. (ERIC document ED 078 017.)

English, F. W., and Kaufman, R. A. *Needs Assessment: A Focus for Curriculum Development.* Washington, D.C.: Association for Supervision and Curriculum Development, 1975. (ERIC document ED 107 619.)

Grabowski, S. M. "Identification and Assessment of Needs." In D. E. Hooten (Ed.), *Proceedings of the Patterns Seminar.* New York: Rochester Institute of Technology, 1975.

Heinkel, O. A. *Priority Determination for Vocational Education Through a Formal Needs Assessment,* Final Project Report. San Diego, Calif.: Research Office, San Diego College District, 1973.

Houle, C. O. *The Effective Board.* New York: Association Press, 1960.

Kaufman, R. A. *Educational System Planning.* Englewood Cliffs, N.J.: Prentice-Hall, 1972.

Kempfer, H. *Adult Education.* New York: McGraw-Hill, 1955.

Ohio State Department of Education. *Needs Assessment Guidelines.* Columbus: Division of Research, Planning, and Evaluation, Ohio State Department of Education, 1974.

Rhode Island State Department of Education. *Needs Assessment: A Manual for the Local Education Planner.* Providence: Division of Development and Operations, Rhode Island State Department of Education, 1975. (ERIC document ED 106 978.)

Rookey, T. J. *Needs Assessment: Needs and Goals — Model: East Stroudsburg, Project NAMES Workbook.* East Stroudsburg, Pa.: Educational Development Center, East Stroudsburg State College, 1975. (ERIC document ED 106 989.)

State Educational Needs Assessment Project. *Report of the State Educational Needs Assess-ment Project (SENAP) of Arizona.* Vol. 1. Tempe: Bureau of Educational Research Ser-vices, Arizona State University, 1970.

Watts, D. A. *Needs Assessment Package.* Atlanta: Office of Instructional Services, Georgia State Department of Education, 1974.

Witkin, B. R. *An Analysis of Needs Assessment Techniques for Educational Planning at State, Intermediate, and District Levels.* Washington, D.C.: National Institute of Education, Department of Health, Education and Welfare, 1975.

Carolyn Watanabe Barbulesco has worked for the past two years as the program planner for the federal manpower program (CETA: Comprehensive Employment and Training Act, 1973) in Sonoma County, California. While completing her master of arts degree in education at the University of Illinois at Urbana–Champaign, she engaged in research on educational needs assessment related to community problem solving.

Many needs assessments may be missing an important ingredient —
public confrontation with those who can respond to the needs.

Evaluating the Assessment: Did Anything Happen After We Left?

Phyllis Safman

Needs assessment activities, long familiar to continuing educators concerned with meeting the needs of adult clients, are usually well-intentioned. While our intentions and techniques may be good, sometimes the needs assessment does not lead to the addressing of identified needs. This happens too often when community needs are assessed. Presented with the assessment findings, community decision makers who can act on those needs may respond energetically, mildly, or they may barely notice those findings.

This chapter describes a community needs assessment process that moved community decision makers into action. The needs assessment was conducted jointly by program development staff members from the office of continuing education and public service at the University of Illinois at Urbana–Champaign and by members of a small rural community. The follow-up assessment of the joint needs assessment process is also discussed.

Background

In 1976 Merekim (a fictitious name), a rural community with a population of 2,600, defeated its school bond referendum. Many other communities, both large and small, also had failed to pass school bond referenda. This recurring problem stimulated the program development staff director from the office of continuing education and public service to begin developing a needs assessment process that would allow a community to review its own attitudes about its public school system. This process contained two special features: community residents were to be involved in carrying out the needs assessment process; and findings from the needs assessment process were to be made known through public forums held in Merekim.

One basic assumption guided the program development staff: Merekim was capable of determining what directions it should take in regard to its educational problems. The role of the program development staff was to assist community members in becoming better informed in order to deal with their school system's problems. Thus, program development staff members, recognizing that Merekim's school system was in financial trouble from the failure of the school bond referendum, were interested in a joint needs assessment process that would help the community understand and cope with its educational problems.

The Joint Needs Assessment Process

The needs assessment process included the following activities: (1) developing a questionnaire to be used for telephone interviewing, (2) identifying and orienting six Merekim residents who would receive remuneration for assisting in the telephone interviewing process, (3) analyzing and summarizing data, (4) developing two public forums where the summary of the data would be presented and discussed, and (5) preparing a final report which would describe the entire process. Merekim residents worked jointly with university personnel in conducting telephone interviews and in providing representatives from the school board, citizens' advisory committee, and teachers' associations, as well as a moderator (all from Merekim) to respond to a summary of the needs assessment data during the public forums. The process was discussed with the superintendent and three educational groups: the school board, the citizens' advisory committee, and the teachers' association. Generally, the groups were favorable with a little reluctance, as the university is sometimes perceived by community members as an invader. However, the opportunity to understand their community's attitudes to education in light of the failed referendum and resulting financial hardship helped the three groups to overcome their reservations about the joint needs assessment process.

Procedures

Questionnaire Development. In order to develop the questionnaire for this telephone survey, the program development staff consulted a national survey (Gallup, 1973) and several state surveys on community attitudes toward public education. The findings from these surveys showed the presence of four major areas of concern nationally and statewide: curriculum, finances, discipline, and communication between school administrators and the community. Because these areas appeared important nationally and statewide, they were considered likely to apply to the Merekim community.

The program development staff, with the help of the survey research laboratory at the University of Illinois, developed a questionnaire to probe these four areas, as well as attitudes concerning the desirability and proper timing for public forums. Open-ended questions were included in order to provide an opportunity for respondents to comment on other issues. Demographic data were also sought. During the questionnaire development stage, drafts were sent to the superintendent and school board for their suggestions and criticism.

Data Collection. Once the questionnaire was completed and the six community persons who would assist in the data collection were identified, the survey research laboratory held an orientation session for all of those involved in the telephone interviewing. At the same time, a selected random sample was drawn from Merekim's telephone directory. Two small population groups, Amish and Mexican-Americans, reside in Merekim without telephones. Two of the community telephone interviewers agreed to hold face-to-face interviews with a sampling from these ethnic groups.

With the completion of interviewer orientation, telephone surveying began and lasted for two and one-half weeks. The program development staff informed Merekim's residents of the telephone survey through the local newspaper and radio stations.

Analysis. Once the data were gathered they underwent computer analysis, including frequency counts and cross tabulations. Frequency counts revealed the number of Merekim residents who held a particular attitude about the school system: 67 percent of the respondents reported that their school system is good or very good. The cross tabulations provided a profile of community residents holding certain attitudes: respondents who said that discipline is a problem in the schools tended to be between twenty and twenty-nine years old, employed full- or part-time, and have no children in school. Once analysis was completed, a summary of the findings was prepared. The summary was concise, informative, and easy to follow.

Forums

Following the analysis phase, two forums, which had been planned by program development staff members and community members, were held in an accessible area of Merekim's downtown district. Local media alerted community residents and provided coverage for the forums. Audience members, the moderator, and the three forum panelists representing the school board, citizens' advisory committee, and the teachers' association were provided with the summary of findings. During the first forum, panelists presented their reactions to the findings and the audience addressed written questions and comments to the panelists through the moderator, a well-known community member.

At the end of the two-hour forum, all those in attendance filled in an evaluation questionnaire that asked their opinions about the proceedings, what they would like to have addressed in the next forum, and their thoughts on future steps. The evaluation questionnaires were analyzed and those items which surfaced repeatedly as important were included in the next forum.

Within two weeks of the first forum, the second forum was held. The second forum allowed for more active audience participation, by encouraging questions and comments after each panelist addressed an issue. Instead of using the written procedure, audience members were encouraged to voice their reactions. This contributed to a livelier discussion and more direct confrontation. At the end of the event, another evaluation questionnaire was given and respondents were asked their opinions on the proceedings and what they would like to see included in the final report, a document disseminated to the community within two months of the second forum.

Findings

The findings from the survey and forums mirrored those of the national and state surveys. Communication arose as a major concern of both teachers and community members who were dissatisfied with the school board's performance. Curriculum turned out to be an area of great confusion. The school board did not understand their career education and bilingual programs. As expected, faculty and community members were concerned about impending budget cuts. Apathy among teenagers and the community was also a concern. Surprisingly, although the telephone survey indicated that discipline was a problem, forum participants and audience disagreed.

Evaluating the Assessment

One year after completion of the assessment, the question of its effect on the school system was raised. To examine this question, an impact study was conducted in Merekim. The purpose of the study was to assess to what extent the needs assessment process affected the educational decision makers in Merekim. Decisions made by the school board subsequent to the needs assessment process were to be identified and examined. Also to be examined were individual perceptions of the process and the effect of the process upon the school board, citizens' advisory committee, teachers' association, and the superintendent.

Literature Review. Prior to designing the impact study, a literature review was conducted, which included the areas of public opinion theory and citizen input for change. The literature indicated that public opinion polls on attitudes concerning education over the last eight years have consistently reflected public sentiment favoring a return to teaching basic skills, enforcing stricter discipline, improving parent/teacher relationships, emphasizing career education, and increasing communication between school and community (Bedenbaugh, 1973; Brainard, 1977). However, the literature on the reliability of opinions gathered in public opinion polls suggests that such opinion is unstable. Reasons given for this instability range from the respondents' lack of understanding of the subject being polled to general public apathy (Converse, 1964, Eriksen and Luttbeg, 1973). Other authors contend that citizen input is essential for broadening understanding and producing favorable results for both the community and decision makers (Elam, 1974; Katz, 1975).

From the literature review two questions were raised that would help to assess the impact of the joint needs assessment process. These were: what effect does public opinion have on decision makers, as indicated by the decisions that are made, and what arouses the public to become better informed and to use new information?

Procedures

Population. Becker and associates (1961) contend that those people who are involved in an activity are in the best position to judge the impact of that activity upon themselves. Therefore, the superintendent, the school board, and the representatives from the citizens' advisory committee and the teachers' association who had participated in the forums made up the information base for the assessment.

Data Collection and Instrumentation. Open-ended, face-to-face interviews were conducted with those twelve people. In addition, supplementary information was gathered from Merekim's weekly newspaper, the school district newsletter, and minutes of the school board meetings. The instrumentation used in the personal interviews was designed to probe the four areas of concern that surfaced during the needs assessment process: curriculum, communication between the school system and the community, finances (particularly budget cuts), and attitudes (especially apathy in regard to morale in the schools and in the community).

Analysis. Data were analyzed according to the four major areas of concern. Variables were grouped into three categories: *influence,* those variables that appeared to influence certain decisions; *process,* those variables that were action-oriented and leading to decisions; and *outcome,* those variables that were the decisions, actions, and consequences of decisions. Four categories of causality linking some action or decision with some part of the needs assessment process were identified. These categories of causality were: (1) causes that could be directly linked to action; (2) actions that could in part be associated with the assessment; (3) those where one could infer a relationship; and (4) those assumed to be related but denied or disclaimed for a variety of reasons.

Findings

The findings are best looked at in light of the two questions arising out of the literature review:

1. What effect does public opinion have on decision makers, as indicated by the decisions that are made? Decisions were made by the school board in three of the four major areas of concern identified in the needs assessment process: curriculum, communication, and attitudes. In the area of curriculum, decisions were made to hire a second bilingual education teacher and a consumer education teacher. To improve communication between the school district and community, a half-time secretary was hired to oversee the regular monthly publication of the school newsletter, which is sent to every household in Merekim. Prior to the needs assessment process, publication of the newsletter was sporadic at best.

While it is difficult to assess to what extent decisions can affect apathy, an attempt was made by the superintendent to boost teacher morale by holding informal small group sessions with all the teachers in the district. Also, one elementary school principal worked with teachers to increase the involvement of parents in the classroom by planning parent/child activities. The small group meetings and the inclusion of parents in school-related activities helped to address the problems created by teacher and parent apathy.

That decisions were made in three of the four major areas of concern indicates that public opinion, as revealed by the joint needs assessment process, does have an effect upon educational decision makers. This tends to undermine the argument of some authors that public opinion has little impact on decision makers. However, in the impact study respondents most often cited the forums as that part of the process that led to changes within the school system. This suggests that the openness of the forums forces the participants to face confrontation, to publicly take responsibility for their views, and thus to be committed to making changes that have been publicly recognized as needed.

2. What arouses the public to become better informed and to use new information? There were several instances reported by respondents and supported in local documentation that indicate that crisis or strong personal interest provide the motivation for people to obtain, use, and interact with information. Farming families vigorously protested the proposed loss of the agriculture program during a school board meeting. Two parents threatened to file suit against the school board for sex discrimination in the athletic program.

Another dramatic example of crisis or strong personal interest as motivation for using and interacting with information can be found in the resolution of one of the four areas of concern, finances. Merekim's school district faced financial disaster because of the failure of its citizens to pass a school bond referendum. Approximately eight months after that failure another referendum was scheduled. For the first time, the school board, citizens' advisory committee, and the teachers' association worked very closely and very hard to persuade their community to vote for the passage of that referendum. With the passage of the referendum, finances were no longer reported to be an area of concern during the impact study.

Strengths

The joint process, which combined the expertise and resources of the university with the resources and interests of the community, made an impact on the school system. While this may be attributed at least in part to the inherent qualities of the process, two additional factors should be recognized:

Time Commitments. Members of the program development staff recognized that projects often take far more time than originally intended. The staff beliefed that in the best interests of the community a tight time schedule should be maintained. Thus, the following schedule was observed:

Initial contact with superintendent and three groups . . . .January 1977
Questionnaire construction, identification of
    community members, training . . . . .Jan/Feb 1977
Telephone interviews . . . . .Feb/Mar 1977
Data analysis . . . . .Mar/Apr 1977
First forum . . . . .April 1977
Second forum . . . . .May 1977
Final report . . . . .July 1977

The program development staff was consistent about keeping its time commitments to the community. What was promised was delivered on time.

Avoiding Preconceptions. The program development staff entered the community with few preconceived ideas. The staff members did not know the problems in the school system, nor did they make assumptions about how the school system should operate. The staff worked with and through the superintendent and the school board, respecting their concerns as long-time residents of Merekim. The staff's openness with all of the groups in Merekim and the staff's refusal to place preconceived ideas upon local residents was consistent. Trust by the community for the university was an essential ingredient that had to be earned and maintained.

Weaknesses

Two areas that might have been strengthened should be mentioned:

Publicity. Even though extensive media coverage announced every step of the process, attendance during the forums was only moderate. More attention might have been paid to working directly and personally with a larger number of teachers, merchants, and church and government leaders in order to stimulate interest. Personal contact is needed for enlisting the support of a wider spectrum of the community leadership.

Planning for Burdens. The joint needs assessment process did affect the school system. However, someone must bear the burden of increased demands brought on by changes. In this instance, that person was the superintendent. The newsletter was now published on schedule, meetings were being held with faculty, resolution of problems over the curriculum meant the hiring of additional staff. These activities became the responsibility of the superintendent. The program development staff was not prepared to assist the superintendent with the increased work load. Both the staff and the superintendent now know that part of the joint process must include a provision for evaluating the possibility for additional work and strategies for handling the work load which is likely to follow.

Future attempts at using or adapting the joint needs assessment process in another setting should consider these contingencies. The Merekim experience indicated that joint needs assessment does have an impact that should be provided for in the planning.

References

Becker, H. S., and associates. *Boys in White.* Chicago: University of Chicago Press, 1961.

Bedenbaugh, E. H.. "A Commitment to Communicating." *Intellect,* 1973, *101* (2349).

Brainard, E. "An Analysis of Public Attitudes Toward Education: The Annual Gallup Polls on Education." *Journal of Research and Development in Education,* 1977, *10* (2).

Converse, P. E. "Nature of Belief Systems in Mass Politics." In D. E. Apter (Ed.), *Ideology and Discontent.* New York: Free Press, 1964.

Elam, S. "Attitude Formation: Direct Experience Best." *Bulletin, National Association of Secondary School Principals,* 1974.

Eriksen, R. S., and Luttbeg, N. R. *American Public Opinion: Its Origins, Content, and Impact.* New York: Wiley, 1973.

Gallup, G. "The Gallup Polls of Attitudes Toward Education, 1969–1973." In S. Elam (Ed.), *Phi Delta Kappa,* 1973, *9,* 202.

Katz, D., and others. *Bureaucratic Encounters.* Ann Arbor: University of Michigan, 1975.

Phyllis Safman is a doctoral candidate in continuing education at the University of Illinois. She is currently completing an impact study assessing the effects of a statewide survey upon legislators, state office planners, and cooperative extension service personnel in Illinois.

A rational, need-reduction, decision-making approach to needs
assessment can improve continuing education programs.

Assessing the Needs of Adults for Continuing Education: A Model

Donald E. Moore, Jr.

Adults typically enroll in continuing education activities because they want to use what they learn almost immediately to improve performance — and they enter learning projects with a background of related experiences and knowledge about the subject matter. These factors have at least two implications for planners of educational programs for adults. First, prior knowledge and experience provide a baseline for subject matter development. Second, if educational activities do not reflect this knowledge and experience, chances are good that adult participants will withdraw, either physically or psychologically.

Adults see themselves as responsible, self-directed, independent personalities. Educational programs will be most effective if they capitalize on these characteristics and incorporate an active search for meaning and relationship between current performance levels and new learnings. The time most adults are willing to devote to educational pursuits is limited because of competing demands from family, occupation, social, and community responsibilities. It is important, therefore, that continuing education activities for adults be timely and relevant. The best way to ensure timeliness and relevance is to identify and analyze the educational needs of potential participants.

Needs and Needs Assessment

In education, the doctrine of needs was introduced by John Dewey in the early twentieth century. Dewey and his followers have been concerned about the "subject-centeredness" of educational planning and have developed the concept of educational need as a way to advocate a learner-centered approach (Atwood and Ellis, 1971). Few educators have questioned or challenged the validity of the concept of needs as a basis for making decisions about educational programming and policy (Barbulesco, 1976).

Educators have incorporated many definitions from other fields into a definition of educational need. Currently, the most popular concept of educational need views need as a discrepancy between an existing set of circumstances and a more desirable set of circumstances. Circumstances are described in terms of knowledge, skills, and attitudes (Knox, 1969); outcomes, results, and achievements (Kaufman 1972); or levels of competencies (Copeland, 1972; Knowles, 1970).

Beginning with Tyler (1950), several authors have described needs assessment activities in some detail. The term *needs assessment* refers to any systematic process for collecting and analyzing information about the educational needs of individuals or organizations. One of the first references to needs assessment in adult education literature was made by London (1960). An important article by Knox (1963), however, expanded the concept of needs assessment for planning and conducting continuing education programs for adults. He suggested that needs assessment projects could be designed to obtain information from the learner as well as from teachers or experts.

State of the Art

A review of the educational needs assessment literature reveals a vast array of definitions, techniques, processes, and models, ranging from individual learners' self-assessments to complex survey, interview, and testing procedures. Some writers suggest that much research remains to be done (Barbulesco, 1976), especially in the areas of: (1) effectiveness of needs assessment techniques and strategies, (2) validity and reliability of various types of instruments and questioning techniques, and (3) cost/benefit ratios for various techniques. Nevertheless, many needs assessment approaches are available that can provide data for administrative and educational decision making. In practice, needs assessments tend to be modest and informal, although those reported in the literature are most often large and complex. The variety of formal needs assessment studies is reflected by the approaches reported by the authors of chapters in this sourcebook. This chapter briefly reviews those approaches, identifies their distinctive elements, and then outlines a model for needs assessment.

Almost all the authors point out the necessity for a formal plan for needs assessment activities. In her chapter, "Components of Major Studies," Carolyn Barbulesco outlined the elements that should be contained in a plan for a formal needs assessment. These elements included a statement of purpose, an identification of the audience for the results, a definition of the general problem area, a delineation of data sources, a description of techniques that will be used for data collection and data analysis, and an outline of how the results will be reported. Barbulesco emphasized that the specifics of a needs assessment plan will differ from setting to setting, but that guidelines for managing a needs assessment project should be useful for any study.

In her chapter, "Adult Learning Needs: From Assessment to Implementation," Helen Veres focused on the management strategy that was used to implement a statewide needs assessment project in New York. In order to overcome potential coordination and communication problems, the state was divided into several regions. Within each region, an elaborate network of continuing education providers was developed to work on the project. According to the author, the participation of these continuing educators in needs assessment activities was a contributing factor in their decision to use the needs assessment results. Project leaders also used the regional network to report the results of the needs assessment activities.

Another management strategy was described by Judith Fidler and David Loughran in their chapter, "A Systems Approach." They outlined the steps of the General Telephone and Electronics systematic approach to needs assessment as applied at the British Columbia Telephone Company. This approach allowed the educator to decide early on if the identified needs are the result of knowledge deficiencies, organizational constraints, or motivational problems. In addition, the approach gave educators an opportunity to provide management with alternative educational packages at different costs to address identified needs.

Availability of resources and the willingness of institutions to commit resources to an educational program are major issues in educational design that are ignored in many needs assessment strategies. In her chapter in this volume, Linda Bock insisted that educators should assess both the needs and interests of potential students and the feasibility of an educational program, by examining resource availability. She described the process by which a small committee assessed the interest of adults in a new adult degree program and worked with faculty in planning the program.

Another approach with a similar emphasis on the marketing aspects of needs assessment was described by Linda Gunzburger in her chapter, "Assessing the Need for a University Program." Again, a committee was used to coordinate needs assessment activities, which included reviewing currently available programs, identifying potential students, estimating their needs, and analyzing feasibility. The emphasis was on demand for a new program in relation to existing programs, rather than on the educational needs of individual adults. Gunzburger suggested that the success of the committee was due to the early identification and definition of decisions that had to be made.

The survey questionnaire is often used for data collection in needs assessment. In "Comprehensive Statewide Needs Assessment of Community College Library Personnel," Robert Means describes the development of a questionnaire by a committee of experts. The questionnaire contained three types of information that were considered useful to educational planners: information about setting, information about education needs, and information about preferences for educational methods. For educational needs, Means described a task-analysis approach which provided detailed information about performance.

A different approach to questionnaire development was described by Wayne Davis, Alan Hull, and Michele Boutagh in their chapter (this volume). The questionnaire would be used with patients before an individualized patient education program would be planned. It was developed in a multistage process that included a literature review and in-depth interviews: a pool of patient characteristics considered relevant for designing educational programs was created; a survey instrument was developed from this pool and mailed to health professionals, who assessed relative importance of the patient characteristics; using the results obtained, the questionnaire was constructed and pilot tested. According to the authors, the developmental process was complex and time-consuming, but provided useful categories of patient characteristics.

Few needs assessment projects examine the use and impact of the findings they generate. In the chapter entitled "Evaluating the Assessment: Did Anything Happen After We Left?" Phyllis Safman described an impact study that took place after a community development needs assessment project. The community development approach was chosen after a small community in Illinois turned down a school board referendum. A community forum was adopted, using the findings of a needs assessment project to examine the reasons for the referendum rejection. After the forum, Safman and her colleagues examined the problems identified to decide if the community development program had produced any changes. The author reported that the program had considerable impact on the problems and led to the desired changes.

Most of the needs assessment activities reported in this volume identify "system-level" discrepancies, that is, deal with needs in the aggregate. The needs of many learners, however, are overlooked by this approach and some learners are unable to relate identified needs to their own circumstances. Beverly Cassara, in "Needs Assessment for the Educationally Underprivileged," emphasized the importance of increasing the ability of learners to assess their own educational needs on a continuing basis. She described a Friere-type dialogue approach to needs assessment that she and her colleagues used with educationally deprived women living in a housing project in the District of Columbia. She reported major success for this approach. Moreover, according to the author, the dialogue approach is useful for all learners, not just "underprivileged" learners.

Each of the approaches described in this volume emphasized a particular component of needs assessment. Such important aspects of needs assessment as developing a plan, establishing a coordinating mechanism, designing alternative solutions, attending to marketing considerations, constructing questionnaires, examining impact, and involving the individual learner directly were highlighted in various chapters. Although each chapter stressed some elements of the process, all authors are working under the assumptions of the same rational, need-reduction, decision-making model.

A Model for Needs Assessment

Program development in continuing education involves a series of decisions that require resolution in order for the process to continue (Houle, 1972; Mazmanian, 1979; Pennington and Green, 1976). As one component of the program development process, needs assessment can be defined in terms of decision making; each of the authors in this volume took this approach. Griffiths (1959) outlined six major steps in decision making: (1) recognize, define, and limit the problem; (2) analyze the problem; (3) establish criteria by which solution will be judged; (4) collect data; (5) formulate and select solution; and (6) evaluate.

The problem that confronts the continuing education practitioner performing a needs assessment concerns the existence of need. The solution to this problem is that a need is defined in terms useful for educational planning. Each author approached needs assessment as a need-reduction process. According to Havelock (1969), the need-reduction process can be viewed as a cycle composed of five stages: (1) a need is felt, (2) the need is articulated, (3) alternative solutions are sought, (4) a solution is selected, and (5) the solution is applied and evaluated. All described activities that assumed need-reduction at the end of application of solution. Most need assessment activity occurs in the stage where the need is articulated. Need reduction assumes a definition of a need as a deficiency.

All the approachs described were rational, in the sense that they proceeded through various activities in a logical fashion. There was reasonable agreement on the sequence and nature of these steps. The following activities were described with varying emphases in all chapters.

Identification of a Problem. The identification or recognition of a problem occurs in many ways, including discussions with affected individuals, potential learners, and experts in the area or drawing upon past experience. This is usually the least systematic and most subjective activity in needs assessment.

Development of a Plan. Although only a few authors expressly indicated the importance of a plan, it was clear that most used a plan. A plan usually describes the purpose of the needs assessment activities, issues related to the problem to be addressed, resources available for needs assessment, and schedule of activities.

Establishment of an Implementation Mechanism. Considerable attention was paid by a number of authors to the development of a coordinating structure to manage the needs assessment process. Committees of content experts, educators, and logistics coordinators, considered essential to successful needs assessment efforts, were described in various forms.

Definitions of Data Requirements. An essential early decision concerns the kinds of data to be collected. Description of issues related to previously identified problems can assist those involved in the needs assessment process in deciding which data to collect as well as in focusing needs assessment activities. Most authors reported that they collected data in three areas: personal characteristics, educational needs, and available resources for educational activities. Only data that relate to identified issues should be collected.

Identification of Data Sources. After deciding what kinds of data should be collected, the data sources are identified. Many sources of data were drawn upon in the needs assessment activities described in this volume. Most studies used more than one data source. The three categories of data sources used were: people, existing records, and published studies.

Collection of Data. Needs assessment data-collection techniques fall into two broad categories: asking people to identify educational needs and inferring needs from existing records and purposeful studies (Barbulesco, 1976). The most commonly used data-collection techniques were survey questionnaires and interview guides, although most authors reported using multiple methods. This is encouraging because of the unknown reliability and validity of many data and data-collection techniques. Some of the other techniques reported included committees of experts, observation, tests, informal contacts, and documentary analysis.

Analysis of Data. Little attention was devoted by most authors to the techniques they used to analyze the data that were collected. This is the weakest aspect of many current needs assessment efforts. Analysis consists of judging and comparing one set of data with another set of data that represents some some standard or criteria. Several authors reported using statistical techniques; others, it seems, used more subjective methods. Few authors mentioned activities related to separating educational from noneducational needs or ranking educational needs.

Reporting. Dissemination of the needs assessment findings to individuals who would use them was described by several authors. In some instances, findings were reported to educational planners or administrators for decision making about educational programming. In others, findings were reported to the learners as part of the prescribed educational intervention. A wide variety of methods was used to report findings, ranging from reports to decision makers to forms that included learners and planners. Cassara and Safman stressed the consequences of needs assessment activities.

Summary and Conclusions

The nine needs assessment activities reported in this volume reflect a variety of approaches to needs assessment, ranging from the formal process used by a telephone company to an informal approach used with educationally deprived women. Although each needs assessment activity stressed different elements of the process, all adhered to the same generic model — a rational, need-reduction, decision-making model.

Individuals concerned with planning and conducting continuing education for adults cannot do a comprehensive needs assessment for every educational activity they plan. Certainly, comprehensive needs assessment is the ideal, but the realities of time, staff, and money are restrictive. The model described here is not ideal, but reflects the actual practice as described in this volume. It is a model that emphasizes techniques at the expense of other components of the process. Despite shortcomings, it appears that the approaches currently being used for needs assessment in continuing education are increasing the participation of adult learners in planning and   nducting learning activities. As approaches to needs assessment become more sophisticated, more effective programs will result and greater impact will be apparent.

References

Atwood, H. M., and Ellis, J. "The Concept of Need: An Analysis for Adult Education." *Adult Education,* 1971, *19* (7), 210-212, 244.

Barbulesco, C. W. "Educational Needs Assessment Related to Community Problem-Solving Programs in Higher Education: Theory and Practice." Master's thesis, University of Illinois at Urbana–Champaign, 1976.

Copeland, H. G. "Need Appraisal." Unpublished mimeographed essay. Minneapolis: Adult Education Department, University of Minnesota, 1972.

Griffiths, D. E. *Administrative Theory.* New York: Appleton-Century-Crofts, 1959.

Havelock, R. G. *Planning for Innovation through Dissemination and Utilization of Knowledge.* Ann Arbor: Center for Research on Utilization of Scientific Knowledge, Institute for Social Research, University of Michigan, 1969.

Houle, C. O. *The Design of Education.* San Francisco: Jossey-Bass, 1972.

Kaufman, R. A. *Educational System Planning.* Englewood Cliffs, N.J.: Prentice-Hall, 1973.

Knowles, M. S. *The Modern Practice of Adult Education: Andragogy Versus Pedagogy.* New York: Association Press, 1970.

Knox, A. B. "Critical Appraisal of the Needs of Adults for Educational Experiences as a Basis for Program Development." Adult Education Department, University of Nebraska, 1963. (ERIC document ED 022 090, 1969.)

London, J. "Program Development." In Malcolm S. Knowles (Ed.), *The Handbook of Adult Education.* Chicago: Adult Education Association, 1960.

Mazmanian, P. E. "Needs Assessment and Objective Setting in Continuing Medical Education Program Development." Unpublished doctoral dissertation, University of Michigan, 1979.

Pennington, F. C., and Green, J. S. "Comparative Analysis of Program Development Processes in Six Professions." *Adult Education,* 1976, *27* (1), 16–23.

Tyler, R. W. *Basic Principles of Curriculum and Instruction, Syllabus for Education 305.* Chicago: University of Chicago Press, 1950.

Donald E. Moore, Jr. is currently chief of the Continuing Education Operations Division in the Office of Academic Affairs, Veterans Administration Department of Medicine and Surgery, Washington, D. C.

*Developing an integrated approach to needs assessment,
program design, and evaluation that will result in
continuous program improvement is the challenge
for the future.*

Educational Needs Assessment: Conclusion

Floyd C. Pennington

This sourcebook has reviewed issues, approaches, findings, and results of educational needs assessment activities. The focus has been on efforts to collect information about decisions that can result in programs that will have an impact on learners and continuing education agencies. Careful needs assessment can have an impact on decisions about the allocation of resources and can elicit support for programs and services. Results of needs assessment activities also have a major impact on persons who provide instructional leadership by providing reasoned descriptions of the clients and their needs.

The preceding chapters present evidence that assessment activities shape subsequent program development decisions. The needs assessment studies reported in those chapters were conducted on adult constituent groups across several segments of the field. However, the frequency and magnitude of needs assessment activities in all continuing education programming efforts remains unclear. Moreover, current literature indicates widespread dissatisfaction with the infrequency of careful assessment activities and the lack of clear guidelines for such activities. Nor is there evidence that all needs assessment activities have a substantial impact on subsequent program development and resource allocation decisions. Yet a growing number of reports on effective needs assessment studies, including those in this sourcebook, make clear that investing time and energy in carefully designed needs assessment activities can have an impact on programs, participant support, and outcome evaluation endeavors.

Many issues affect needs assessments. Some educational programs are not well designed because the needs assessment was inadequate or nonexistent. Well-designed programs must deal directly with specific, achievable performance changes that are important to the adult learner, are amenable to an educational intervention, and can be readily documented beginning with a careful description of current and desired behaviors. The process of generating this description and understanding the magnitude of discrepancy between the current and desired situation is the core of an effective needs assessment strategy. Selecting the type and amount of educational intervention likely to bring about the desired change requires informed decision making. That decision making is enhanced by relevant data that can be acquired through needs assessment activities, which can provide a clear understanding of whether the need is one of proficiency or is situational and whether it requires administrative or environmental solutions. Results from needs assessment studies can help curtail the application of anemic interventions by zealous continuing education practitioners to problems of major complexity and substantial difficulty. Even when clear descriptions of current and desired circumstances provide sufficient baseline data, it is often difficult to separate the impact of those data from the continuing educators' common sense and instinct as well as the chance opportunities that often contribute to correct design decisions in the absence of real data.

Continuing education practitioners conducting needs assessment studies will find social and behavioral science research methods useful. During a needs assessment study, independent and intervening variables can be isolated, described, and understood. The magnitude and potential impact of these influences on program outcomes can be predicted. Practitioners who engage in systematic needs assessment activities are advised to acquire basic research skills and select personnel who can complement their proficiencies in the assessment techniques that are selected.

Understanding the relationships between education and action is a major accountability question for continuing education practitioners. Continuing education programs typically have multiple goals, several of which can be thoroughly described prior to the program if a reasonable assessment has occurred. To assess the impact of any continuing education program requires a clear understanding of the entry behaviors of the learners. Evidence of entry behaviors is best collected prior to educational interventions. Isolating specific behaviors that can be addressed by educational interventions provides an index against which to assess outcomes with control or comparison groups. In many instances, neither control nor comparison groups can be used and the data collected on potential participants serves as the baseline against which a program's success is judged. Needs assessment data used as longitudinal data permit more careful inferences of the probable impact of the educational program on the participants and make possible comparisons with nonparticipants.

Data from multiple sources serve the continuing education practitioner well. Some data sources are more trustworthy than others. Some data are more robust than others. Collecting observations from multiple role perspectives or with more than one data collection technique provides for the important confirmation and cross validation required for subsequent program development activities and allocation of the required resources.

A fairly comprehensive framework for needs assessment is useful. Not every variable related to a problem or situation can be studied in detail. Using a variety of informants enhances the likelihood of identifying the most important components of the problem. Such a framework would include data from potential participants, faculty, and others essential to a potential program's success. Special care would be taken to get the most informative data possible. If observation of actual behavior is impossible, simulations might be used. If surrogate observations are not possible, more indirect measures might be sought through self-report techniques. Few needs assessments can carry the burden of providing the continuing educator with all the information required to make all the right decisions for an entire program. Consideration of key components of problems and situations by isolating the important variables and describing them as fully as possible promotes sound programming decisions.

A desirable needs assessment study requires effective dissemination channels to the persons who can make the necessary programming decisions. It should give some indication of the validity of data-collection instruments and the priorities of need likely to lead to the required short-term as well as long-term action. It should compare results with accepted relative and absolute standards derived from normative data or excellent practice. These standards are usually derived from sources external to the data being collected from clients in an ongoing assessment activity.

Most educational needs of adults are not absolute. The concept of a need for an adult learner depends on context. Behavior is affected by the environment and learning implies a change in behavior. Assessing learning needs requires analyzing both individuals and the situation in which they interact. Needs will change in number and magnitude as the individuals and their environments change. Understanding need in this context will require both subjective and objective information.

A persistent issue in needs assessment is who can best ascertain individuals' needs. The perspectives of both the learners and others can help in identifying gaps. Individuals often have a wealth of information and understanding concerning their needs. Because learning is essentially an internal process, only learners themselves decide to learn and to act upon their learnings. Persons other than the learner (program planners, experts) can in some cases specify objective standards to which individuals can compare themselves in order to ascertain the nature and magnitude of their need. Where such standards are absent or minimal, persons who are knowledgeable in a given area might supplement or even provide alternative reference points.

Needs can change rapidly, even during educational programs. The literature suggests that the needs assessment process should be continuous, perhaps taking place at regular intervals during a program. The literature (Knowles, 1970; Miller, 1964, Tyler, 1950) also advocates the use of behavioral objectives more as prescriptions than as instructional devices, thereby setting serious limits on the possibility of ongoing needs assessment.

It should also be pointed out that needs of a system are not the sum of the needs of the individuals within it (McMahon, 1970). Although systems have problems, they cannot be educated. What a system is said to need is basically what an observer needs or wants for the given system. If the performance of a system is to improve, the individuals within the system must act upon themselves and upon their system.

The importance of value considerations is an issue when the continuing education practitioner is faced with the question of choosing among conflicting or contradictory needs. The question of which needs should be dealt with among the nearly infinite number and which course of action fo meeting needs should be selected can be perplexing. The concept of need has no meaning without a set of norms, without which it cannot be identified. The value question emerges when trying to decide who sets the standards or whose standards will be accepted.

Needs assessment literature often implies that the diagnostic procedure is politically neutral, that it must assume the values of the client system, or that the so-called self-fulfillment models are self-justifying. If it is assumed that the continuing education practitioner is the final arbiter of high-priority needs, does this constitute an imposition of the educator's value system upon the learner? If it is assumed that needs assessment is solely the function of the continuing educator, how does this affect self-determination of the individual? Manipulation by educators may be determined by the extent to which they justify their teaching on the ground that it is good for the learner, by the extent to which the student is allowed to participate in educational planning, and also by the extent to which educators expose their own assumptions.

Institutional goals influence the kind of needs assessment done, as well as the outcome when the needs have been analyzed and ranked for priority. Needs are not well defined and obvious to any observer. Perception of individuals' educational needs is mediated by the qualitatively and quantitatively limited perspectives of observers, including their goals and philosophies.

This sourcebook should make clear the importance of needs assessment as an integral part of designing instruction for adults. However, more work needs to be done to strengthen the definition and theory. Needs assessment will be served by carefully designed studies that analyze the extent and type of impact needs assessments have had on subsequent program development activities.

References

Knowles, M. S. *The Modern Practice of Adult Education: Andragogy Versus Pedagogy.* New York: Associated Press, 1970.

McMahon, E. E. *Needs of People and Their Communities and the Adult Educator: A Review of Literature and Need Determination.* Syracuse, N.Y.: ERIC Clearinghouse on Adult Education, Syracuse University, 1970. (ERIC document ED 038 551.)

Miller, H. L. *Teaching and Learning in Adult Education.* New York: MacMillan, 1964.

Tyler, R. W. *Basic Principles of Curriculum and Instruction, Syllabus for Education 305.* Chicago: University of Chicago Press, 1950.

Floyd C. Pennington is the director of the continuing medical education program at the University of Michigan in Ann Arbor. He spends a substantial amount of time on formal and informal needs assessment studies to provide a basis for sound program decision making.

Index

New Directions Quarterly Sourcebooks

New Directions for Continuing Education is one of several distinct series of quarterly sourcebooks published by Jossey-Bass. The sourcebooks in each series are designed to serve both as *convenient compendiums* of the latest knowledge and practical experience on their topics and as *long-life reference tools.*

One-year, four-sourcebook subscriptions for each series cost $18 for individuals (when paid by personal check) and $30 for institutions, libraries, and agencies. Single copies of earlier sourcebooks are available at $6.95 each *prepaid* (or $7.95 each when *billed*).

A complete listing is given below of current and past sourcebooks in the *New Directions for Continuing Education* series. The titles and editors-in-chief of the other series are also listed. To subscribe, or to receive further information, write: New Directions Subscriptions, Jossey-Bass Inc., Publishers, 433 California Street, San Francisco, California 94104.

New Directions for Continuing Education
Alan B. Knox, Editor-in-Chief
1979: 1. *Enhancing Proficiencies of Continuing Educators,*
       Alan B. Knox
      2. *Programming for Adults Facing Mid-Life Change,* Alan B. Knox
      3. *Assessing the Impact of Continuing Education,* Alan B. Knox
      4. *Attracting Able Instructors of Adults,* M. Alan Brown,
         Harlan G. Copeland
1980: 5. *Providing Continuing Education by Media and Technology,*
         Martin N. Chamberlain
      6. *Teaching Adults Effectively,* Alan B. Knox

New Directions for Child Development
William Damon, Editor-in-Chief

New Directions for College Learning Assistance
Kurt V. Lauridsen, Editor-in-Chief

New Directions for Community Colleges
Arthur M. Cohen, Editor-in-Chief
Florence B. Brawer, Associate Editor

New Directions for Exceptional Children
James J. Gallagher, Editor-in-Chief

New Directions for Experiential Learning
Morris T. Keeton and Pamela J. Tate, Editors-in-Chief

New Directions for Higher Education
JB Lon Hefferlin, Editor-in-Chief

New Directions for Institutional Advancement
A. Westley Rowland, Editor-in-Chief

New Directions for Institutional Research
Marvin W. Peterson, Editor-in-Chief

New Directions for Mental Health Services
H. Richard Lamb, Editor-in-Chief

New Directions for Methodology of Social and Behavioral Science
Donald W. Fiske, Editor-in-Chief

New Directions for Program Evaluation
Scarvia B. Anderson, Editor-in-Chief

New Directions for Student Services
Ursula Delworth and Gary R. Hanson, Editors-in-Chief

New Directions for Teaching and Learning
Kenneth E. Eble and John Noonan, Editors-in-Chief

New Directions for Testing and Measurement
William B. Schrader, Editor-in-Chief